WAR & PEAS
INTIMATE LETTERS FROM
THE FALKLANDS WAR
1982

HMS *Ambuscade's* Crest.

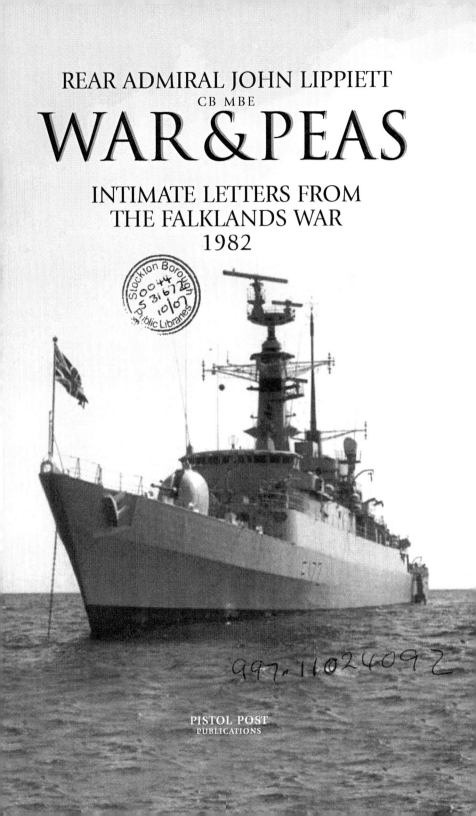

REAR ADMIRAL JOHN LIPPIETT
CB MBE
WAR & PEAS
INTIMATE LETTERS FROM THE FALKLANDS WAR 1982

997.11024092

PISTOL POST
PUBLICATIONS

WAR & PEAS
INTIMATE LETTERS FROM THE
FALKLANDS WAR 1982

First published in 2007 by
PISTOL POST PUBLICATIONS
The Watergate, Ratham Lane, Bosham PO18 8NH
E-mail: john.lippiett@falklandswarletters.com
Website: www.falklandswarletters.com

ISBN 978-1-904459-26-2

Distributor
MARITIME BOOKS
Lodge Hill, Liskeard, Cornwall PL14 4EL
Tel: 01579 343663
Website: www.navybooks.com

Produced and printed by members of
THE GUILD OF MASTER CRAFTSMEN

Cover Design by RPM
Book Design and Typesetting by Cecil Smith
Set in Giovanni Book

Printed and bound in Great Britain by
RPM PRINT & DESIGN
2-3 Spur Road, Quarry Lane, Chichester, West Sussex PO19 8PR

Dedicated
to those fighting for their country
in 1982 and since,
and their families back home.

CONTENTS

ACKNOWLEDGEMENTS

I was prodded into writing this book by friends who considered there was merit in drawing together an account of a naval war of twenty five years ago, balancing the diary-like letters from the South Atlantic with the commentary from home from the worried family. This war of 1982 may have been the last war where letters played the only form of correspondence, being in the days before mobile telephones, text messages and emails. Today's instant communications produce their own advantages, and indeed disadvantages, to today's service personnel and their families. But despite the slow method of sending the messages backwards and forwards, the sentiments are much the same: from the fighting front, a factual account, normally underplayed regarding danger, with a yearning to return to loved ones. From the home front, a brave face, stories of family and home (and garden!), and a desperate wish to keep the recipient out of danger's way. Therefore I see our letters here to be a reportage of events of a quarter of a century ago that will be utterly recognisable to today's servicemen and their families. Above all, I acknowledge the stresses borne today by our hard-pressed servicemen and women and their long-suffering loved ones.

Having decided to tell the story of HMS *Ambuscade* and the Falklands War in this way, I quickly realised that I needed to put the details of our daily operations within the context of a factual background obtained from more official records. I am therefore most grateful to Captain Chris Page and Lieutenant Commander Jock Gardner of the Naval Historical Branch for their support and their interest in the project. Yet more help was at hand from my Captain of that time, Commander Peter Mosse, who kindly lent me his Night Order Book. This was the manner in which he recorded by hand each evening his instructions for the conduct of the ship while he slept. Inevitably it is disjointed, as was his sleep, but it does create a lively and authoritative account of his view of the immediate operations. Additionally, Peter has been good enough to read through the script and provide me some very good pointers for improving my commentary on the events. Our combined memories have produced the best possible recollections of what were sometimes muddled days, but I daresay there will be readers who will have differing views of the what actually happened! The one area of our activities that I felt I had least knowledge of was the helicopter operation while away from the ship. For this reason I turned to Lieutenant Phil Henry, the Flight Commander, and I am grateful for his assistance. Through my research I have been able to create what I believe is a unique summary record of the daily life of a ship in this war.

I found I needed some clear maps of the Falkland Islands, for some of the narrative gives names that are difficult to locate on an ordinary atlas. I should like to acknowledge, with thanks, the splendid assistance I received with the three maps printed in this book, specially drawn by the Design Office, the Public Works Department, Falkland Islands Government.

Finally, I joined *Ambuscade* without a camera, so have had to rely on photographs provided by other members of the ship's company. Again, Peter Mosse has been kind enough to provide me the vast majority of those published here, but I should also like to thank Alf Symonds, Steve Griffin, Steve Frith, David Marchant, and Dave Rowlands. The majority of the photographs are on display on the excellent website of the

HMS *AMBUSCADE* Association
(www.ambuscade.org.uk),

and I thoroughly commend readers to have a look if they can, and to learn more about this active association.

Lieutenant Commander John Lippiett MBE.
1982

PREFACE

THE WAR ARRIVED unexpectedly and with a speed that was almost inconceivable. A diplomatic fuss over some scrap metal dealers in South Georgia ("Where?" asked most people) escalated over the coming weeks into a full scale invasion of the Falklands Islands, a British Dependent Territory eight thousand miles from the UK. With extraordinary dexterity, British forces geared up to recapture the Islands while diplomatic activity attempted to find a peaceful solution. The Ministry of Defence named the mission Operation CORPORATE and the Royal Navy took the lead. This is my story, as an individual, and as the second-in-command of a frigate, told through my letters back home.

Our training and whole outlook was oriented in Cold War thinking towards a North Atlantic NATO and Warsaw Pact conflict. But we expected the philosophy of deterrence to work, and to be honest, we didn't expect actually to fight! Perhaps deterrence and diplomacy would work as the Naval Task Force sailed southwards. The sinkings of the Argentine Cruiser *General Belgrano* and then HMS *Sheffield* changed our perceptions. This was for real.

Whatever our expectations, we were military personnel and highly trained and motivated. Our preparations for fighting were intense and thorough. For HMS *Ambuscade*, the ship I joined in April, we had our moments of excitement and played our full part in the operation, though we missed the hottest action right at the opening phase. We returned unscathed but battle weary. There were tragic deaths and grievous injuries on both sides during the war, but most of the combatants came back home, to the relief of their families. The scars of the battle remained for some – and do so even now – but for the lucky majority life returned to its routine norm, leaving all a little wiser, a little sadder, and probably a lot more professional in their business.

There was little time to stand back or take stock of the situation, and certainly no time to worry about what was to come in the weeks ahead. Not so with our families who saw us all go off to war, as countless generations have done over the centuries before. Their worries, exacerbated by the lack of real information and the inevitable rumour mill, were much harder to bear. The strains back home were very considerable, so this is also my wife's story, told through her letters to me. With a daughter aged 4^1/$_2$, a son just 2^1/$_2$, and expecting our third child in November, this war is just as memorable to her as it is to me.

Our letters have sat in boxes in the attic until now. Re-reading them, our memories are re-ignited and the progress of war can be seen through the understatements, the forced jollity, and the determination not to worry the other. Unable to report all the operational goings-on from "Down South", for reasons of security, my letters home could often only hint about the operations, and I would invariably wish to play down events so as not to exacerbate the inevitable worry at home. Likewise, Jenny only rarely displayed her full angst in her letters. Her emphasis was on home life, the trivia of the daily routine, and the progress in the garden as spring turned to summer. All these were essential factors in helping me get through those weeks of war.

Putting the letters together in chronological order shows how out of synch we were with each other's knowledge of the day's events. We often didn't get letters from the other for several weeks and then they would come in a bunch, though occasionally with one or two missing from the sequence.

In gathering this book together, I see that the lack of sequence can be confusing, so I have published the letters on the date of

Garden Peas in Westbourne, West Sussex.

their writing and preceded each day with a summary of that day's activities. I have given some timings, principally to illustrate the 24 hour nature of our operations and also the length of time that some evolutions took. I have also included a summary of the predominant weather conditions on that day, by giving an average wind direction and strength, the sea state, and also the miles steamed in that day. (One nautical mile = 2,000 yards, just over one land mile). For those readers unfamiliar with wind strengths described in the Beaufort Scale and the sea state code – as used in our shipping forecasts – I include tables at the back. In summary, Force 6 is a strong breeze and Force 8 is a gale. Sea State (SS) 4 is described as "moderate" with waves of 8 feet and SS6 is "very rough" with wave heights of 20 feet. Our Ship's Log recorded SS9 on occasions and the code describes this as "phenomenal" with waves over 45 feet! I have then added some specific quotations from the Daily Orders which I signed each day, to give the reader an idea some of the instructions that were put out to keep the ship's company up to scratch – and sometimes amused. I hope these daily summaries provide the backdrop for my narrative back home.

I have tried to remove – or certainly reduce – the military's constant love of acronyms, but I have let the reader in gently to some of the abbreviations I have used to sharpen the text. I have included a glossary at the back to help those who get a bit lost! However, my letters are full of the family nicknames, so I had better introduce the family and their names here and now:

> **Jenny**, my wife.
> **Louisa**, our daughter, was known as **Wee**
> (after she couldn't pronounce her name, but
> would say Weesa). **Marc**, our son, was known
> as **Bee** or Bumble.

> The unborn baby was nicknamed **Alfonso**
> (why I'm not sure!), and was born Oliver in
> November 1982. **LMA** = Louisa, Marc and Alfonso
> My wife's sister, Eleanor, was known (and still is!)
> as **Bim**, but also as **Toots**, just to complicate
> matters.

> Our cocker spaniel was strangely named **Jerbil**,
> known as **Jerbs**. (It, too, became pregnant over
> this period). Sometimes also called Toad.........
> oh well, sorry about all this!

I have attempted to make all other friends, acquaintances, and fellow naval personnel anonymous by inserting their initials in place of their names. No doubt there will be those who spot themselves and others who will be thankful not to! Readers may note that HRH The Prince of Wales appears as a name within the letters. He took a very active interest in the Navy's engagement in the South Atlantic, and showed a touching anxiety for his contemporaries and their families left back in the UK. I had served with him as a fellow Commanding Officer in mine-sweepers some six years before the war, and his kindnesses in

Easter 1982 before leaving the UK.

1982 were typical of his real concern for members of the services. I therefore considered I should not expunge the references to him in our letters.

Our home was in Westbourne in West Sussex. A modernish end of terrace house which we had recently extended, we revelled in gardening and were putting lots of efforts into developing our small garden into something worthwhile: we had a stream in the front garden and a newly established vegetable plot in the back. Inevitably hard up on the financial front (which comes through in our correspondence), we were determined to head towards self-sufficiency on the vegetable and fruit front. Hence the emphasis on peas!

Rear Admiral John Lippiett CB MBE.
The Watergate
Bosham, West Sussex. 2007

Gibraltar, April 1982.
A Barbary Ape poses on the Rock with
HMS *Ambuscade* alongside the Naval Base.

CHAPTER 1

JOINING
IN GIBRALTAR

FTER MY nine month staff course at the Royal Naval College, Greenwich, it was time to return to sea. I was a 33 year old Lieutenant Commander, a trained Warfare Officer with experience in a wide range of ships varying from an aircraft carrier to minesweepers. But I had not served in a Type 21 Amazon Class frigate, so when I joined HMS *Ambuscade* in Gibraltar on 23rd April I was stepping into a different class of ship, one with very specific characteristics. I had much to learn, and fast, for I was joining to take up the post of the Second-in-Command, known formally as the First Lieutenant or Executive Officer (XO). Informally the nickname for this was Number One or The Jimmy.

There were eight Type 21s, built in the 1970s as a light escort with a general purpose capability. With the upper works built of aluminium, and powered by gas turbine engines, they were very fast and manoeuvrable, and had a reputation for being the sports car of the Fleet. Rather disdained as not being of conventional build (they were commercially designed rather than by the Royal Corps of Naval Constructors), the ships' companies developed a very distinctive, slightly piratical, character within the 'Twenty-One Club'. Each ship's company numbered only 170, considerably smaller than previous sizes of crews. Everyone onboard worked harder, took more responsibility and got more job satisfaction because of it.

Armed with a 4½ inch gun on the forecastle, the Type 21s also had a first-generation and rather obsolete anti-aircraft short-range Seacat missile system mounted aft, complemented by 20mm Oerlikon short range guns on the bridge wings. Anti-submarine torpedoes in tubes were placed on the upper deck. The frigates carried an impressively capable Lynx helicopter that could carry anti-submarine torpedoes or anti-ship Sea Skua missiles, and this flew from the flight deck at the stern. With radars, sonars to detect submarines, and electronic warfare equipment to detect the enemy's radar and communications, these ships had a pretty good all-round fighting capability.

Ambuscade had been sent down to Gibraltar to act as Guardship and to reinforce the garrison's magazines with ammunition from the UK, these having been emptied by the Task Force that had already sailed southwards to Ascension Island. We were due to be in Gibraltar for three weeks before returning to the UK for an intensive operational sea training programme. On that basis, I took over my duties from David Childs, who had completed a very successful tour and deployment beyond Suez. Had my Captain known what was to happen next, he never would have accepted the change of his deputy at such a crucial time!

27th April
    Lieutenant Commander Lippiett joins
    HMS AMBUSCADE in Gibraltar.

28th April
    0130 HMS AMBUSCADE receives orders to
    prepare to become Guardship for
    Ascension Island. Next 3 days spent
    storing and ammunition for war.

Westbourne, West Sussex.   *29th April*

My darlingest man,

I was rung yesterday to tell me you are about to sail south, so I emptied the sherry decanter and went to bed with my book on Nelson. He was exhibiting his weakest side – the one with the empty arm – and was no possible substitute for you. Clever man to take your whites [*uniforms*] – did you *know?* I had no feelings that you might go; which is probably just as well, as otherwise I might have drugged your Earl Grey. I know that you may well not get to the hot spots, but I find myself pitifully wondering as I water your baby grass whether you will ever see it again...

My darling John, you are my entire focus for living and for loving, and everything I do right down to cutting my toenails is done with you in mind. I talk mentally to you all the time, and I find it hard to face up to the fact that the phone is not going to ring and I am not going to be able to tell you how nice I was to your mother when she dropped in unexpectedly for lunch yesterday. I know it would be like this at times whether or not the Falklands thing had happened, but I feel your absence so much more poignantly – and I nearly died this morning when I misheard "Here is the news" as "Here is a news flash"! I shall have a lot more grey hairs when you return.

I feel incredibly drippy, but I shall not drip over you. Do your bit, my darling, and know that wherever you are and whatever you are doing, we are all thinking of you and loving loving loving you and living for the moment of your return. Take every care of your most precious self. You are absolutely everything to me. J xxxxxxxxxx

30th April
Total Exclusion Zone established around Falkland Islands

HMS Ambuscade.   *Thursday 30th April*

My darlingest Jenny,

0845 and post closes at 0900! First news is (and you may already have it by telephone from others) that we won't be back as planned, surprise surprise... We are naturally sworn to keep our plans secret, so I can say no more, though you are clever enough!

Don't worry, all is entirely well and we are safer than crossing the A27.

They've been having torrential rain and storms here whilst we have been basking, but I brought the good weather here and yesterday – a long day at sea – was lovely.

David C [*the XO from whom I was taking over*] will stay in the chair for the immediate future (though we ring the appointer later today) and I will gradually take over and back up as required – not totally satisfactory but best in the circumstances.

Have been completely out of the news since leaving UK – haven't heard a thing. Re-routing of Economist would be greatly appreciated!!

The situation is obviously very fluid indeed so can make no guesses at all, except the certain knowledge that we will be back safely. Censorship will be in force after we leave here – perhaps that will be my job onboard... Naturally a <u>real</u> doc joins us so all my vast training is being discarded.

Happy 1st May from afar. [*Our sixth wedding anniversary*] I adore you beyond all imagination. Be brave during this period, but don't fret. All my love to you.

HMS *Ambuscade* alongside in Gibraltar, April 1982.

HMS Ambuscade.   *The Glorious 1st of May!*

My darlingest J,

<u>Lovely</u> to hear you this morning – so clear that you might have been next door – what a lovely thing that telephone is. <u>And</u> a letter yesterday – super as ever.

I haven't a minute to myself, there is just so much to do, to get settled in and on top. A sound team at the moment to back me up, so I'll be relying on them to keep things running whilst I catch up.

Meanwhile, we paint <u>everything</u> grey – no numbers or names on the side – imagine painting the tall black mast!

David C was seen off after lunch today in good style, I hope. Had to lead him on a final run ashore last night (not that I could spare the time). [*A 'run ashore' is an evening in local pubs or the like.*]

All looks good – very happy with situation – nothing like dropping in at deep end!

What a way to spend our anniversary – not happy for you I fear because you have all the time in the world to think, whereas I have so little. Anyway, thank you for the six most happy years of my life – I really couldn't have enjoyed them more; you are the most fabulous wife and I adore you constantly and utterly. I look forward to the next 66 at least! Kiss for the children, and tap on tum for Alf (and Toad!). All my love on this great day.

HMS Ambuscade.   **Sunday 2nd May**

My beloved wife,

And so it continues, non-stop. Popped ashore this morning to Church with a few others – Matins – rather pleasant, but otherwise it's all go onboard.

I'm enclosing a few bits and pieces in that there's not really time to describe everything. The handout (that will test you) is so you can see what we look like – except that we don't, because <u>everything</u> that you see there is now grey – top to bottom. Numbers painted out et al.

The will is a requirement for everyone onboard and needs depositing with bank or solicitor (former I should think). <u>But</u> not needed, please note!!

An old chum joined today to take passage with us for a short while – JH – we joined up together, but hadn't seen each other since cadets. He may well ring you in due course with a bit more news.

Later... Just had your phone call after supper – isn't that machine lovely! I'm glad that you are keeping busy (but remember that ½ hr lie down!) for it's the best way to be. Don't get worried or miserable. Isn't it nice that you've got such <u>nice</u> children with you – it would be horrid if they were terrors all the time! (Is Marc sleeping better? – I've just seen my postcard to him and I've spelt his name with a k. Unforgivable, shows what a hurry I wrote it in and also how long it's been since I last wrote the name. Do you think he'll ever let me forget this mistake?)

Darling one, I long to hear all your news, even the smallest detail, for it all brings you much closer to me. If my letters are brief and unsatisfactory, bear with me, and I <u>promise</u> you no-one will censor the <u>in</u>coming mail!!!

Take great care – wrap <u>yourself</u> and LMA in cotton wool and don't stir till I get back. All my love and more.

CHAPTER 2

THE FIGHTING
COMMENCES

IN OUR SNATCHES of news bulletins, from the BBC World
Service, it was apparent that the diplomatic efforts to reach a
peaceful solution had been unsuccessful. Without a
declaration of war (was one needed, for the Falklands had been
taken by force earlier in the year?) the reality of our entry into
war came on 1st May with the RAF bombing of the runway in the
Falklands, in order to prevent the Argentine air force from using
it, and the bombardment by RN ships of the enemy positions on
land.

And then the tempo of the war stepped up momentously with
the sinking of the Argentine ship *General Belgrano* by the
submarine HMS *Conqueror* on 2nd May. We were stopped in our
tracks by this news, but despite the regrettable loss of 368 lives,
it was seen as an early success to reduce the threat to our large
Task Force off the Islands. If this was to be such a desperate fight
then we needed to gain the advantage in such a way. As it turned
out, this was to be the end of the threat posed to us by the
Argentine surface fleet, although we believed their submarines
continued to patrol.

3rd May

HMS AMBUSCADE sails from Gibraltar, heading south at 18 knots. 0830 exercise Action Stations. Conduct anti-aircraft exercises against RAF Jaguars flying out of Gibraltar. Emergency Stations [*when the ship's company closes up to fight a major disaster*], and a helicopter flying exercise. Ship darkened overnight, with merchant ship lighting rigged. Total silence on all emitters (radars and radios etc)
(Wind South westerly, Force 4, Sea State 1. Miles steamed:277)

FROM DAILY ORDERS:
PREPARATIONS FOR WAR

a) <u>Censorship of Mail.</u> After we sail all mail will be censored. Further instructions will be issued after sailing. Until then no post will be accepted after the final collection. (0715)

b) <u>Securing for Action.</u> A considerable amount of work has already been completed securing the ship for action. When in NBCD States 1 & 2 the ship is to be fully secured for action, but at other times relaxations may be made. After sailing the bogey time for the fully secured for action state is 15 minutes. Mattresses will be left in position on individual bunks, but they are to be lashed.

c) <u>Name Tallies.</u> It is particularly important at this time that name tallies are worn and are legible.

Jenny's Viewpoint

When John left for Gibraltar, he took a minimum of his things with him, as he flew out on the Tuesday and was due back in Plymouth on the Saturday. He needed the few days of the return passage from Gibraltar to take over from the previous First Lieutenant, so that the ship would be ready to start the dreaded Work-Up, or training for war, with Flag Officer Sea Training. This was always arduous and tough, but its value was about to be proved in a real war.

I was going to take the rest of John's gear to Plymouth on the Saturday – things like pictures for his cabin, books, clothes, a radio and various other necessities like nail scissors! We kissed goodbye, but I had no idea that I would not see him again for three months, and that during those three months he would be in very real danger. I think I was glad that I did not know this at the time of our farewell.

After what seemed like quite a long time of hesitancy and uncertainty over how the Government should react to the invasion of the Falklands, once the decision was made to re-take them by force, everything happened very quickly. Ship after ship seemed to be dispatched south: both warships and ships commandeered from the Merchant Navy, right down to some Roll-on, Roll-off ferries. By the time I heard that *Ambuscade* was to head south too, I was expecting to hear this news, so was prepared for it. In many ways, I was glad: at that time, we all expected there to be a diplomatic solution to the conflict, but if there was to be a Real War, then most of the members of the Armed Forces wanted to take part. After all, they trained for it all the time, but they never really knew how effective they would be. That could only be proved in the arena of a genuine conflict.

Many of us left behind were undecided as to the merits of this conflict. The wholehearted desire of the people of the Falklands to remain under British rule and not to be a province of Argentina was a strong argument in favour of war. On the other

Sailing south, HMS *Ambuscade*'s wake.

hand, were these small, remote islands worth the price of British lives? Some cynics pointed out that having territories in the South Atlantic gave us a claim on any possible mineral wealth in Antarctica, and that the war was being driven by potential commercial gains. More, however, saw the cynicism to be on the Argentine side, with President Galtieri attempting to defuse domestic riots by re-claiming the islands which Argentina had always said belonged to her. It was indeed a very popular move when he made it, but his timing was disastrous. Had he waited a few more months, until after the carrier *Invincible* had been sold to Australia, *Hermes* had been decommissioned later in the year and other defence cuts heralded in the Nott Review had taken place, Britain could not have sent the Task Force that she did, and the islands would have remained under Argentine control.

Whatever people in Britain felt about the conflict, everyone was kindness itself to me and to most of the other wives with husbands in the South Atlantic. Stories abounded of bank managers extending loans to wives who had no access to cash because their husbands had gone off without transferring money to them, or of cars being mended for nothing, because the mechanics felt sorry for the wives. One of my own encounters with civilians who wanted to help concerned the young owner of a smart clock shop in the village. I had decided to think positively and to get John a barograph, something he had always hankered after, as a particularly special birthday present to celebrate his return from the war. I asked in the shop if he had any, or could get hold of one. "There used to be a lot around, but I haven't seen any for some time. However, I will move heaven and earth to make certain that you have a barograph before your husband gets home. I admire our Forces tremendously – in a way, I would like to be called up to fight myself!" And he did get me a barograph, and it is still recording the daily atmospheric pressure – though these days there is never the pressure that there was during the war!

EMERGENCY MEDICAL OPERATION

With hindsight, it was inevitable that we should turn left instead of right as we exited the Straits of Gibraltar, for we were heading to Ascension Island, situated in the South Atlantic. This British territory had become an essential staging post for the South Atlantic Operation, being around halfway towards the Falkland Islands, and possessing a runway on its rugged, moon-like terrain. There was little else on the island, but there was a real worry that the island might be attacked by Argentine forces, so we sped southwards to be the Guardship.

We sailed covertly, with no radars emitting, and in radio silence, with no transmissions of signals. This was to deny the enemy the ability to track our movements. From leaving Gibraltar to the end of hostilities we invariably sailed fully darkened at night with no navigation or steaming lights and no upper deck illuminations, and 'deadlights' on all doors and scuttles (portholes). Occasionally we would turn on navigation lights that were configured to make us look like a merchantman. We would alter course away from other shipping and fishing vessels so as not to be identified, We were as invisible as we could make ourselves and relied solely on visual look-outs to detect any other ships in the area.

Later on that first day on passage south, the Medical Officer – a young Surgeon Lieutenant who had just started his naval career having completed his medical training – came to see me. "We have a serious medical problem, sir," the Doc reported, "and we must return straight away to Gibraltar to land the man." In peacetime this would have been the natural course of action, but as we were heading to war this was not an option. We discussed the problem, which was that a stoker had had a fight onshore the previous night in Gibraltar, if memory serves me right, and had cut his hand. He now had blood poisoning which was getting worse, and stood to lose the use of his hand, or arm, or even his life. The young Doc was not confident about his capability to operate, so we set about reading his medical manuals together. After all, had he not been onboard, I was the designated Medical Officer as XO, and I had completed a two-day course to equip me for all eventualities. Had I not learnt how to inject oranges and to sew up pork chops?

Having studied the options, we went to see the Captain and after a debate we decided to break radio silence to get medical advice from Gibraltar before operating. This we attempted but failed to get through, so we then set to work in the tiny sickbay onboard. Assisted by a young Leading Medical Assistant, the Doc started the operation with me in attendance. It was to be a local anaesthetic, and my role was to engage the patient in conversation throughout the operation to keep his eyes (and mine) from straying to the gory mess as his hand was cut apart, and also to turn the pages of the medical manual that the MO was consulting as the operation progressed. (Both I and the patient found this rather disconcerting!).

I learnt every single thing there was to learn about that young man as we searched for conversation over that next hour and a bit. No detail of his life was missed as we explored every aspect of it. But the operation was a success, and the patient recovered to play his full part in the war ahead of us. For us in *Ambuscade*, this was the first action of the war, notched up by the newest individual onboard.

4th May
> Passage south at 17 knots. Action Stations exercise 0830-1030. Drills 1630-1800. Ship darkened and silent overnight (Wind south westerly, light. Sea state 2. Miles steamed: 382)
> HMS SHEFFIELD hit by missile.

FROM DAILY ORDERS:
PREPARATIONS FOR WAR
a) <u>Ammunition Whips</u> for emergency supply are now rigged throughout the ship and will remain so until further notice. These whips are not under any circumstances to be used for any other lifting and are to remain in their present positions.
b) The amount of paper on notice boards is to be reduced to essential notices only.
c) <u>Be vigilant!</u> If you are working or relaxing on the upper deck, cast your eyes around occasionally for a periscope, There are likely to be foreign submarines taking an interest in our passage south.

We heard via the BBC World Service that HMS *Sheffield* had been hit by an Exocet missile launched by an Argentine aircraft. Twenty-one sailors were killed, and more injured. This body blow, the first of a fair number, made a deep and lasting impact on us all. It weighed particularly heavily on the senior officers, who felt yet more seriously the responsibility to fight successfully and to bring their ship's company back alive.

Certainly the loss of *Sheffield* caused every single individual to redouble their efforts in training, which still continued around the clock as we sped south. One other practical outcome from the loss of *Sheffield* was the realisation that there was very considerable danger from the spreading of thick, acrid smoke when a warship is on fire. The importance of smoke control had always been acknowledged, but now we hastily constructed makeshift smoke curtains in the passage-ways through the ship. These would be closed in action to add a barrier, in addition to the watertight doors, to keep smoke contained in the area of a fire. It is interesting to note that smoke curtains are now standard fit in our warships today; lessons from the Falklands conflict, learnt the hard way through loss of life, have not been forgotten.

Jenny's Viewpoint

HEAVY
CRUISER

The sinking of the Argentine submarine *Belgrano* and the loss of life was a terrific shock, and made us all question again whether war was the right way to go. Then, however, *Sheffield* was sunk, and there was no going back. I remember sitting in the bath and half-watching the television news in the bedroom next door. The announcement about *Sheffield* had me popping up like a jack-in-the-box, and I nearly fell out of the bath. This was Real War, and so many people that I knew and loved were now in real danger.

Despite being pregnant, I started to lose weight, which worried the staff at the ante-natal clinic. I remember being told to go and eat as many chip butties as I could manage – a repulsive thought, particularly since I was endeavouring to eat as healthily as possible on behalf of the new baby. We always referred to it as 'Alfonso', but we never knew the sex until he was born. Scans in those days were very limited both in number and range, and they could not make out the detail of scans these days. I was very concerned that the baby would be influenced by the vast rushes of adrenalin and fear that seemed to course through me on hearing the news on many days, but to our relief and joy, all seemed well in the end.

Westbourne, West Sussex.   *4th May*

My darling John,

I wonder how many of these letters I shall be writing before we meet again. There is such an unreal quality to this separation – the feeling of not knowing at all what the future holds – and I hate having nothing to look forward to. If it looks like going on a very long time, I trust you will make a little hole in the ship somewhere which will ensure that you have to return to Portsmouth.

But what a fabulous difference those phone calls made! Bim, who had heard me in tears on the Friday because I had failed to get hold of you and thought you were sailing the next day, found me grinning right round to the back of my head on the Saturday, after talking to you! We went to the Craft Market in Emsworth and I bought myself an anniversary present – a very pretty necklace which Bim spotted as being Just Jenny. It was nice to have a bonus for being separated! And incidentally, I hope separation pay is substantial – we had a statement showing us to be £85 overdrawn before your pay went in. What a good thing we can save up now – pace new necklaces! (Mrs. Lippiett says Pace is Latin and here it means 'not counting'. I wouldn't expect a mere sailor to know this.)

Other letters do <u>not</u> include one from you, which is a substantial disappointment. However, knowing that one is on the way is an inducement to get out of bed after a sleepless night thanks to Marc's nocturnal ramblings. But at least he drops off in the afternoons, which seems to work out quite well! I have had your mother to lunch <u>twice</u> and feel incredibly virtuous.

Bim stayed the weekend and dug over the empty garden ready for peas, sweet corn, courgettes, marrow and cucumbers to go in as soon as the frosts stop. We have masses of each, and ten globe artichokes and a thousand purple sprouting all doing very nicely, thank you – but not a peep from a bean or a pea. However, the potatoes have appeared, so I shan't despair yet. The garden is so immaculate that it is boring – I even mowed the lawn today, which makes me feel that I have assumed responsibility for the whole thing, including the car exhaust. So your capable wife is now in control, but I'd so much rather sit about being told to rest for at least half an hour!

Our social life ticks on with lunches and teas and coffees and phone calls – something every day, and as I was asked straight out if I was pregnant when out to lunch recently, the word is spreading. Everyone is gratifyingly delighted for us and astonished at how flat I am – in fact, I'm a lot flatter than when you left, so I'm glad I have an antenatal appointment on Monday to make sure it's still there! I'm sure it is – it's just that I have obviously lost some extra pounds as a result of eating and drinking less.

How I would love a glimpse of your life at sea. The news reporters with the ships all seem very impressed, and we get good coverage of events. I hope you know where your life-jacket is, and don't forget to duck when you see something strange coming at you. It all sounds rather hotter than I would wish.

The children are being sweet (most of the time!) though Marc asks several times a day when you are coming back. Louisa won a prize today for getting a row of stars – the prize was a miniature tractor which was quite clearly an unclaimed toy from some terms back! L is obviously doing very well, and has gained in reading skills already. Interestingly, she has to learn to recite ABCD… so I am singing it to her in a version I learnt at a Bishop's Party for Clergy Kids when I was about 6. I also play tedious games of ball with Marc, and allow them both to cover themselves with finger paint, and reckon I am being a Good Mother.

I'm off to have a bath. Big big kisses to you – and I shall have to sit against the taps because I shall be watching the news in the bedroom through the bathroom door!

*   *   *

Later: nearly fell out of the bath on hearing the news of HMS *Sheffield*. How unutterable. What can I say? I love you and love you and love you, and I live for the moment of your safe return.
J

WORK UP

'Passage to Ascension' sounds a pleasant occupation, but ours was at the other extreme. We worked around the clock to train in every aspect of our business. We had embarked some specialist sea training staff from the renowned organisation called FOST (Flag Officer Sea Training), and they put us through our paces and sharpened our skills.

We had stripped out the ship of all its peacetime luxuries while at Gibraltar. Normal kit was limited to absolute bare necessities, while the Wardroom silver, wooden furniture, pictures, books, music equipment, golf clubs and much more was landed into containers, not to be seen for months. Every mirror and any remaining glass was secured with a cross of heavy tape so as not to shatter if the ship suffered an explosion. Carpets were lifted and bare steel was exposed wherever possible so as to reduce the risk of fire. Any 'tiddly' features such as the two coloured motor boats, the white bollards and the black mast and funnel top were painted warship grey so as to maximise the camouflage effect. We even painted over our pennant numbers F172 from the ship's side and stern, so as not to reveal our identity.

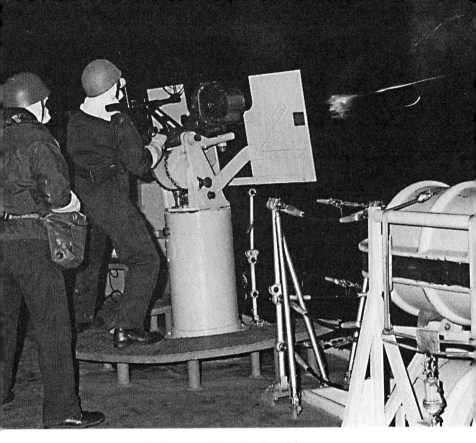

Night exercise 20mm Oerlikon firing.

5th May

Passage south at 18 knots. 0600 Emergency
Stations exercise
0830-1030 Action Stations. 1700-1900
drills. (Wind north westerly, light. Sea
State 2. Miles steamed: 376)

6th May

Passage south at 18 knots. 0830-1030 Action
Stations. Drills throughout day. (Wind
northerly, Force 4, Sea State 2. Miles
steamed: 400 miles)

```
FROM DAILY ORDERS:
PREPARATIONS FOR WAR
```
<u>Noise :</u> Remember that submarines detect us by
our radiated noise. The amount of radiated
noise, our "noise signature", depends on four
factors:
a) Flow noise made by the ship through the
    water and which is dependent on speed.
b) Propeller noise, also dependent on speed.
c) Machinery noise. Running machinery
    transmits vibrations to the hull.
d) General noise: loose beer kegs, gas
    bottles, ladders, unsecured tools, blocks
    and whips, etc.etc. transmit sound through
    the hull.

    All of us can contribute to reducing
    GENERAL NOISE by making sure that the
    equipment, tools and stores are stowed
    correctly, thereby avoiding noise shorts
    which transmit vibrations to the hull.
    With the ship at slow speeds this may
    make the difference between a submarine
    detecting us or not.

Westbourne, West Sussex.   *6th May*

Darlingest husband,

It was such a treat to have your letters on the mat today, and
it helped so much to have even such scanty contact. I'm afraid I
am not being a good wife and smiling at the world bravely – I
wear my heart on my sleeve and I can't pretend that I am not
vitally concerned for you, and incredibly upset by the news from
the South Atlantic. We are all shocked and stunned by the news
of the *Sheffield,* and tonight's news of the loss of two more Sea

Harriers brings it all home yet again. I weep for the wives and pray for you, and long to have more letters from you assuring me that you are still there. You'd better have a photo taken clutching the latest Economist! I shall send them on to you, but they will all be smothered with chocolate and marmalade, as they tell me much more of what I want to know than anything else can! I do miss my military advisor!

I hope that Iain may be able to tell me lots of interesting facts when we all go to lunch there on Sunday. Your mother had asked us, but she rang earlier this evening to say that something else had come up, so I rang Liza and she instantly said, 'Come up on Sunday', which was exactly what I was hoping for. We go to J on Saturday, and today we had lunch and tea out, so you can see that I have virtually no time at home to sit and fret! Alfonso will be frenetically sociable, and will drive us dotty with his desire to go out all the time…

I went to Chichester yesterday in the morning, and we have an amazingly healthy bank balance! It must be your back-dated 6% – long live pay rises! I might get the exhaust done.

They have announced the list of casualties from *Sheffield*. I was frightfully worried for RC, but evidently they hit the kitchen and <u>not</u>, as they originally said, the Ops Room. There seemed, sadly, to be a lot of cooks involved. In case you haven't heard, it was 20 dead and 27 injured, but only one of the latter is on the danger list. I now understand why you would most like to be on *Broadsword* or *Brilliant* – they have been explaining that only Sea Wolf could have stopped the missile. Couldn't you transfer – do a swap with someone? At least it sounds as though you have a lot to do, which must be rather fun – though I hate to think of the job you will have restoring your lovely brass rails when you get back. It had better be a punishment duty! And what's the point – I thought radar was colour-blind?

I must remember to tell you about your wicked dog. She got out last Wednesday through the fence where the forsythia joins the panelling (I discovered this by following her the next morning), and she disappeared entirely. Sam [*next door's dog*] was nowhere to be seen, and though I drove round and round through the village, I couldn't find her and went to Knight and Lee to get Louisa's dress material. Ron caught her flirting in the road with Sam at about 11o'clock, and tied her up in the garden, but when I got back it was obvious that Jerbs had been Done. Sinister marks on her back and a sinister smile on her face. So £7.50 at the vet's after seeing Eileen and going dancing – what a day! – and the worst part of it all is that it has prolonged her season and she's obviously still busy flirting 8 days later. CB brought a huge labrador who was staying with her when she came to lunch on Sunday, and we had fearful scenes from Jerbs telling this thing that she was already engaged to someone else. We had a jolly nice lunch, but C seems to be very boot that her husband's prolonged absence means she can't start No 3. I suppose we are awfully lucky to have got ourselves organised in that direction – though with people saying that you may not be back before Christmas, I sometimes wonder. Ah well, time will tell!

Frost tonight – help! We have two freesias up. I must go out in rain and hail and cover them. The chrysanthemums arrived today, but the weather has been <u>foul</u>. I do love writing to you, but must stop indulging myself or you'll never get any work done. Darling, darling man, I love you more than you will ever know. Take care. Jxx

7th May
0830-1030 Action Stations. Drills, night flying exercise. Passage south at 14 knots. Ship in Defence Watches, watch on, watch off for next 4 days. (Wind northerly, Force 4, SS2. 389 miles)
Exclusion Zone declared by UK up to 12 miles off Argentine coast.

FROM DAILY ORDERS:
PREPARATIONS FOR WAR
The ship goes into Defence Watches today to
prove the system. The routine is as
follows:
0800-1300 Port Watch
1230-1330 lunch
1300-1800 Starboard Watch
1730-1830 supper
1800-0100 Port Watch
0030-0130 snack
0100-0800 Starboard Watch
0730-0830 Breakfast

CROSSING THE LINE
We will be crossing the line on Sunday at
about 0200, but have received the following
message from King Neptune:

DICTUM EQUATORION
I, King Neptune, do decree
That those who sail upon the sea
Aboard the Warship Ambuscade
Shall have no charge against them laid,
For I have heard by way of mouth
That they have business further south.
And so, safe passage I declare
My dolphins shall escort them there;
Ere they return to this domain
My worthy court shall entertain.
NEPTUNUS REX

RN DEPENDANTS FUND
Cost: Officers: £3 pa, Ratings: £1,80 pa.
In the event of your death your dependant
receives a lump sum of £2000 to cover
funeral expenses etc.

Refuelling in calm seas from *British Tamar*.
The author on the left in white overalls.

8th May

0500 launch helicopter to search ahead for our tanker. 0715-0930 Replenish Liquids (i.e. fuel) "RAS(L)" by the astern method with MV BRITISH TAMAR. Transfer mail for home. 0803 Sunrise. 1100-1430 Anti submarine exercise with HMS ONYX. Passage south at 18 knots. (Wind NW 3, SS2. 372 miles)

9th May

HMS AMBUSCADE CROSSES THE EQUATOR. Church service on Flight Deck. Hands to bathe (1155 and 1625, for both watches). Sea 82°F. Passage south at 19 knots. (Light airs, calm. 426 miles)
Clocks onboard put to Zulu time (Greenwich Mean Time). This is then the time zone used by all UK forces throughout the hostilities.

FROM DAILY ORDERS:
KING NEPTUNE'S TEMPORARY MEMORANDUM 1/82
Further to my proclamation
Giving special dispensation
I do extend an invitation
(Follows here an explanation).

Dolphins, your fine ship escorting,
Foreign contacts not reporting,
Suggest to me an item sporting
To which I trust you'll be resorting

At Nil degrees declination
(By Obs or DR navigation)
Your swimmers shall take up their station
For Piscean recreation.

Fifteen-thirty don't be late
Neptune's dolphins thee await.   41
                              NEPTUNUS REX

Stopped on the Equator for hands to bathe. Scrambling net and boarding ladder down starboard side. Ship painted entirely grey, with all distinguishing marks removed.

HMS Ambuscade.   *Sunday 9th May at sea*

My darlingest wife J, Where do I start? Time has flown and my feet haven't touched the deck; nearly 2 weeks onboard and yet it seems like yesterday that I flew out. I'm glad that this should be the way, but no doubt it's the reverse for you, and will continue to be so. I'm only too aware that I have plenty of company and activity, whilst your life remains around the kitchen sink and the children with little to relieve it. However, I hope that you do manage to keep busy, whilst ensuring that you put your feet up for a rest daily!

Lots of questions. How are you all, how's Wee at school, and Marc at play school, how's Jerbs (with litter??), the garden, the bank account! Alfonso, Westbourne, Sussex, Britain, the world??? We listen to the World Service news at every opportunity and this is often our first news of what is going on.

The news flash about *Sheffield* came as an enormous shock and when I announced it to the ship's company immediately it was a particularly sombre XO. I understand that the list of casualties has been published at home, but we haven't seen it. I'm thankful that the final casualty list was comparatively small – a tribute to the way the men fought the damage and to the design of the ship. The incident did much to sharpen up the standards here – which were pretty sharp beforehand anyway.

Censorship is in, and I have to censor a number of senior rates' mail and the officers'. Not a pleasant task, and time-consuming.

I've tried to ensure relaxation takes place this weekend to help everybody – very important. Hands to bathe this morning in a very appropriate position – water was beautiful. We had a quiet 'Saturday night at sea' last night – enjoyable, the food onboard is outstanding, so I'll have problems…

It's a good ship, with a nice feeling. I'm happy with the Wardroom and ship's company. Friendly and happy. I spend as much time just wandering around getting to know people and taking an interest in their work. That's the fun of being No. 1 – you can go anywhere/talk to anyone without trespassing.

As I said before, JH has been with us for this trip and will be flying back. I'll ask him to ring you with any extra news.

I can say that we are in the South Atlantic – just crossed the line at midday and swam across it!! Stopped the ship (twice in fact, to allow both watches) and dived in. It was delicious – warm to hot, but refreshing and not too salty. 10,000 feet below us was the closest land – the deepest I've swum in. Morale onboard is pretty high despite a bad past programme and an unknown future. My job, as I see it, is to keep that going despite what could be a pretty frustrating period. I'm optimistic!!

Before I turn in (Sunday ½ midnight) – BFPO677 is (or might be) better than BFPO Ships…

More tomorrow – meanwhile, I adore you, long for you, and am ever your own. J

Hands to bathe.

Westbourne, West Sussex.   *Sunday, 9th May, 1982*

My darling, We're all shattered – children asleep and me just waiting for the news before going to bed – after a super day chez McNeil. We had lunch and then went to Windsor for a walk and a go on some children's roundabouts and trains beside the river – all great fun, and as the children supped and bathed there, it wasn't even a pain when we got back! So you can see that we all gallivant madly as soon as your back is turned, and you'd better stay away until we have exhausted all our friends – next week.

I may say that the Foreign Secretary [*Francis Pym, a distant relative of the family*] is personally interested in your whereabouts and activities – he and Valerie rang Mummy two nights ago to tell her how much they had enjoyed a night off at the theatre – they went to see '84 Charing Cross Road', presumably on her recommendation. She said that he sounded as though he had nothing in the world to do except talk to her, and he asked after you – remembered your name – and wanted to know where you were. I expect he will intervene in your programme, and you'll be sent to the South Pacific soon, out of reach of the Argentines.

Prospects for peace advance and recede with monotonous regularity, and I don't think anyone believes in it any more. There's a general feeling 'Let's get on with it and to hell with world opinion'; we are all sick of the skirt-dancing by Argentina. I find myself waking up saying 'Costa Mendes' or 'Perez de Cuellar' [*Argentine politicians*], and I dream about it all night long. Last night I dreamt that I was responsible for issuing a new puzzle consisting of letters inside a square – something like a Rubik's cube – and if you got all the letters in the right order it told you the names of all the warships in the Task Force. I awoke feeling desperately guilty!

Forty tons of loose flab has been burnt off today during the London Marathon, so perhaps we'd better take up Marathon running to get our waistlines back to 32"?? The first chap home did his 26 miles in 2 hours 9 minutes.

And after that piece of useless news, I shall go and have a bath and make myself lovely for Alfonso's first presentation of himself to the doctors at S. Richard's tomorrow. We are lunching with your mother, who reports that Peter has 'flu and Thomas now has chickenpox. Maggie sent us a picture of Nathaniel on his birthday (literally!) and he looks <u>sweet</u>. Purr, Coo!

CHAPTER 3

ASCENSION

OUR ORDERS had been to stay at Ascension as the Guardship for some weeks, or possibly even months. However it was clear to most of us by the time we arrived that we could expect to be continuing south, so our arrival at this island staging post gave us a short period at anchor to draw breath. We were concerned that even the anchorage could be attacked, so we kept guard by bringing our defensive "Operation Awkward" into action, keeping the Operations Room and weapon crews closed up and alert. A conventional submarine, HMS *Onyx*, was also at anchor, and, knowing their lack of facilities, we had them over to have a shower and a meal, and to watch a movie. Luxury indeed for the 70-odd crew, who were accustomed to very basic living conditions onboard their cramped submarine.

10th May
    0550 Flying exercises, 0708 crash-on-deck
    exercise. Hands to Emergency Stations.
    Ship's Company closes up in Defence Watches
    (watch on, watch off). 1700 anchor off
    Ascension Island. Main engines at 20
    minutes notice and armed guards posted on
    the upper deck for Operation AWKWARD (Wind
    SE Force 4, Sea State 3. Miles steamed 322)

First sighting of Ascension Island.

HMS *Onyx* at anchor, Ascension Island.

FROM DAILY ORDERS:

a) <u>OPERATION AWKWARD</u> The most likely threat to
the Ascension Island is some form of
sabotage attack. We will therefore assume
Awkward State 3 on anchoring this evening
and all subsequent occasions of anchoring.

b) <u>DARKEN SHIP</u> The ship is to be fully
darkened from half an hour before sunset
until sunrise. No smoking is allowed on the
upper deck between these times.

c) <u>GASH</u> The routine for ditching gash will
have to be strictly regulated from today,
especially as there is a Russian
intelligence gatherer in the immediate
area. The aim is for gash to be ditched in
the dark and to have sunk by daylight. All
gash is to be ditched between 2200 and
0100. Tins are to be flattened and if
possible sacks should be weighted. No gash
is to be ditched at anchor or when within 3
miles of Ascension Island or when within 5
miles of the AGI.

Westbourne, West Sussex.   *Monday 10th May*

My darling one – watching HMS *Bristol* and *Liverpool* leaving for
the Falklands on the box brings the whole misery of the situation
back again – waving, weeping families wondering if they are to
face the ultimate tragedy – it's all too horrid.

Let us instead concentrate on Alfonso, whom I actually saw
on the ultrasound screen today! He was leaping about and he
looked just like the pictures – a wiggly sort of thing, with a huge
head and his legs all tucked up. 12½ weeks according to the nice
scanner-man, who froze various pictures on the screen while he
measured the head and the length. It's all so exciting! And he's

all there now, so I don't have to worry about strange viruses and things. I am told that this delivery should be much easier – I have a magnificent pelvis, but my uterus seems to have taken time to get going! So if you're not here, it won't be as traumatic as before.

We had lunch afterwards with your mother, who thrives happily. However, news from Barnstaple is not good – Thomas appears to be suffering from rheumatic fever and they are very worried about him – can't keep his temp. below 104°, and he has been into hospital with it, poor chap.

I went to the bank after lunch and found that I could pay off most of my Barclaycard as well as yours, plus £50 for Louisa's school fees, so things look up. It has been a v. hot day, so things are looking up in the garden too – first peas and French beans through, and I am hardening off the sweet corn and leeks ready to go out. All the raspberries have now decided to live; but sadly two of the chrysanthemums which arrived on Friday have keeled over. The blossom on the apple tree will have to be photographed for you!

When I collected Louisa she brought a little friend home for tea. No sign of her parents, so I got her phone no. from Mrs. Norton and rang through when we got home to find that her grandfather had been waiting for her but she had gone off without a word to him! She's a nice child and fitted in well – lives with her grandparents as parents divorced – but it was all a bit much today as I felt exhausted after all morning at S. Richard's and the afternoon in Chi and walking Jerbs. She is <u>still</u> in season, which wrecked our plans for her to play with dog McNeil – and she got out again today when the playing child was collected and someone rang up simultaneously. She was gone for 2½ hours, but this time I shall leave it, and she can be spayed if she is found to be in pup. The injection she had last time prolongs the season, it seems, and I cannot stand any more of this!

Sarah and I have immensely long gossips on the phone, and we are both lunching out on Thursday – me plus Marc and she plus 3 and 1-year olds. We have been in touch over the launching of a new postcard by the Post Office showing a mail delivery to

Ambuscade in Devonport. It sounds incredibly dull to me – why not fearless helicopters winching down from stormy skies? – but they are having a jamboree and have invited us mere wives since none of you can be present as originally planned. So providing L eventually puts her phone down so that I can ring her up, I intend to go down on Thursday 20th, taking Louisa from school at midday, have the jolly on the Friday and hopefully meet a lot of other wives plus a few aged naval captains who are beyond going to sea, be dutifully circumspect about your doings to the Press, radio and television (we have been asked to do this!) and return here perhaps via Somerset on the Sunday. It will make a nice break, I trust.

What a lengthy letter! News in brief: *Sheffield* has finally sunk. There are only 14 people left on next term's Staff Course at Greenwich. DC's job had already been filched by someone else when he got back! Northwood was given weekend leave – it is thought in preparation for a long haul in the near future. They cancelled 'I remember Nelson' on TV in favour of a debate chaired by David Frost on the Falklands. I should have thought the former was the more inspiring.

Darling, darling man, I do love you so very much. I spent most of last night thinking of you and how utterly wonderful you are. Come home to where you are appreciated! I miss you quite horribly. Love, love, love J xxxxxxxxxx

HMS Ambuscade.   *Monday 10th*

I fear this is a scrappy letter with a minute here and there. Action started at 5 this morn with exercise Helicopter ditching, followed by ex. Crash on deck at 7… And so it goes on. My daily wear is now white overalls, antiflash and lifejacket – rather different to normal. Whilst out of danger, we are still ready for anything and working defence watches (½ ship's company closed up all the time).

Now afternoon, and I must go to walk around. I'm longing to

hear from you – hopefully letters this eve and then quite frequently for quite a time. Every little scrap of gossip is fun. Any photos of yourself? ? I've got the few I took from the album but only 1 of you. Why not go and have a portrait taken?

My darling, I'll close this now so that it gets into the first sack ashore. I think that even you would be surprised to know how much I love you. I long to be back with you – take great care until then (no fainting in church!) and stay cheerful – it's the only way to be. I am (it's my job!) and that might help you. All my love to you, my dearest girl.

PS. I suggest you don't discuss inferences of the letter with other wives, trying to wring out of you what we are doing – it would only cause confusion and upset – act vague!!!

Transferring stores to HMS *Onyx* by ship's boats.

ENGINE PROBLEMS
WITH THE HELICOPTER

The helicopter's flight into Ascension when taking the Captain ashore for briefings is worthy of note, for at the moment of touchdown the Port engine failed. This was identified by the Flight Commander, who got out to investigate odd readings on the port engine's instruments. He immediately beat a brave retreat to search for a fire extinguisher whilst indicating to the pilot to shut the aircraft down. The ensuing task of replacing the engine saw four members of the Flight being flown from the ship and a replacement engine being supplied by airlift, courtesy of a passing Wessex 5 helicopter from one of the supply ships late in the afternoon of the 11th. The Flight rapidly carried out the engine change overnight using whatever lighting they could borrow, and managed to get it ready before the daylight faded on the 12th. They then took the opportunity to get a few well-deserved beers, their last for some months. The Senior Maintenance Rating, who had been overseeing the engine change, took the opportunity to drive down to the village of storage containers that festooned the side of the runway at Wide Awake airfield, looking, as he described it, like a scene from a Vietnam war movie with military equipment scattered everywhere. The result of his sortie was reflected in the first weapon status report we later made on joining the Carrier Battle Group; it detailed the 8 General Purpose Machine Guns and nearly 60,000 rounds of ammunition that we had acquired that day!

On return from their run ashore to the salubrious PANAM building (a two-storey wooden framed building used as a storage facility with air conditioning provided courtesy of holes in the sides of the building) which had been requisitioned as flight accommodation, the team bedded down on flour sacks only to be woken up at 0500 to be told to get airborne at first light to carry out the engine check test flight. This was to be done before landing on *Ambuscade*, which had just received orders to sail south. Once airborne it became apparent that there were further problems with the engine test flight, so the Flight Commander decided to land on the ship and continue the tests during the journey south. Extraordinarily, the starboard engine, up till then the serviceable one, failed at the moment the helicopter landed. The ensuing passage south had the Flight very busy for the next week replacing and then trying to match up the 2 engines. Ashore and in peace-time conditions such a task would be demanding but fairly routine; however, at sea in cramped conditions, rough weather, and with limited facilities, the Flight did a superb job in sorting these problems out successfully.

11TH May
Operations off Ascension, flying and transfers
all day. Our helo has engine failure on
landing, and is unserviceable on Ascension
airfield. Engine changed during day. Soviet
Intelligence Gathering Auxiliary (AGI) in
our vicinity. Patrolling overnight. (Wind
SE, Force 3, Sea State 3. Miles steamed: 64
miles)

We had changed our watch-keeping routine by this stage and the ship's company now worked in Defence Watches, half being on watch for six hours at their war fighting stations, while the other half carried out their routine tasks, or fed and slept. This routine was the set pattern thereafter, slightly modified later by 6/6/4/4/4 hour routine, until 5th July. But the on-off watch system was constantly being broken, first by our exercises and then later by 'Action Stations', when the whole ship's company closed up, either at their weapons and sensors or at their machinery controls, or at their damage control stations scattered throughout the ship. Having the entire crew closed up ensured that, if hit, there would be enough personnel to mend the damage and to keep the ship afloat and fighting. That was the theory, anyway!

Both before our arrival in Ascension and thereafter, we were to practise all eventualities with gusto: firing the guns, flying the helicopter and exercising crashes on deck, fighting fires and floods, exercising anti-missile defence procedures, training for first-aid emergencies... you name it, we practised it.

HMS Ambuscade.   *11/12 May*

My very own darling J,

One card and three letters yesterday – fantastic to hear from you and all your news. What a treat mail is – it really does boost everyone's morale. We expect to get mail at least 3 times a week for some time now so... Keep writing, and I'll try too. Late now, and 6 o/c start tomorrow with plenty to do. Don't think that we'll be too bored; many things that I haven't got around to yet and must.

How is / was the scan? I'm a bit worried to hear that you're losing weight – can this be true? Hope all's well and that Marc is letting you have some sleep at night. Naughty boy – tell him from me. Nice to hear of Louisa's prize, do say a big well done from me. Did they get their p/c's from Gib – sorry there aren't any more – don't really exist out here!

Jerbs (pregnant!)... has she got a permanent grin from ear to ear? Poor you, what an extra worry to have to cope with. Did you have a nice Sunday with Iain and Liza? Hope so and that he reassured you well.

All is going well. Captain told the news of programme, however vague, to the ship's company this morning and they took it quite well. Basically all (or most anyway) are resigned to being away for a long time and getting on with whatever they are told to do with no fuss. Have good spirit onboard and must maintain it. Still can't say where we are, but must be fairly obvious. I understand some wives have rung the Advice Offices the RN have set up and have been told exactly – but we're not allowed to say, lest it confirms or denies it!

Had a letter from my Ma – she obviously thinks that she must hover around you to look after you and report back to me that you're OK.

Darling one, getting mail off first thing in the morning, so will turn in now. I think of you every moment that I'm left on my own. Our union is perfect, even at thousands of miles away. We know what we are each thinking and take pleasure in it. Go on talking to me whilst you're cutting your toenails, for I'm listening to you. I haven't cut mine yet for I haven't any scissors!!

Jenny, I adore you and long for the eventual return. Keep cheerful, be brave, give the kids my love and a cuddle. All my massive love is for my darlingest wife. J

HMS Ambuscade.   *12th May*

My very dearest, darlingest J,

A Free letter! And you can collect these from GPO and send them to me free – so lots and lots and lots of them please! Isn't that kind of them – the only perk so far. No letters since the first burst of 3 so I look forward to them.

Things have changed from a couple of hours ago and this may well be the last letter for quite a time. It's a fast-moving world here and the situation changes from minute to minute. As ever we can't say anything of our movements, but you're quite a clever girl. Indeed your guess is as good as mine at the moment, because we haven't actually been told anything. The fog of war indeed! It might be worth ringing the enquiries office in Pompey 755212 to see if they can tell you anything – I don't know the amount of info they are giving away, but it might be more than we are allowed to. It might also be worth treating even that with a pinch of salt for I have heard some strange rumours of what has been said.

It seems a somewhat unreal world, to be in this situation after a matter of a few weeks. One minute all is peace and calm, tending the peas and loving my family and the next being far far away and heading for uncertainties. But what is certain is that we shall return (perhaps sooner because of the present change, than before – who knows!) safely and having done whatever is required of us. There are tens of thousands of people in exactly the same position, so it's not as though we are being singled out. Indeed there could be future stigma attached to <u>not</u> being involved!! What a silly world it is! Anyway, spirit is high, we have a good team and I am happy leading a nice bunch of guys.

I shall be over the moon when we return, and shall whip you (no, not quite) away for a super holiday to rejoice in our reunion. It is the greatest joy to me that I found you, got you to marry me, and that our marriage has gone from strength to strength. It really does get better daily – even in absence. Keep on talking to me – I am with you – and will be with you bodily (hooray!) in the not <u>too</u> far distant future. Keep smiling – look after yourself. All my love to you, my Jenny. J

HMS Ambuscade.   *12th May*

My dear Louisa,

Your first grown-up letter from Daddy. Can you read it? If you find it difficult, ask Mummy to help you.

It is now late at night – nearly midnight, and I have been up and working hard since six this morning. Hard work so the day goes very fast. Are you still enjoying school? Well done for getting a prize – aren't you a clever girl. I'm very proud of you, and look forward to coming to see you at school one day. How are the dancing classes going?

Be good, and look after Mummy very carefully whilst I am away. She is the very best of mothers and you are so lucky. I'm in my ship now, sitting at the desk in my cabin (which is really a room without windows!) Thank you for your letter – I loved it. Do draw me some pictures and send me some more letters. Take great care. With love from Daddy

Dear Marc,
Here is Daddy's ship. Can you draw one like it?

You must come and see it when I get back; I'm sure you will find it exciting. Enjoy the summer, I expect to see a brown berry of a boy! Help Mummy and sleep all night! What a lovely time we will all have together when I return. I long for it. Love from Daddy

CHAPTER 4

ASCENSION TO
THE
FALKLAND ISLANDS

12th May
> 0830 R/V with HMS ANTELOPE who has
> Argentine Prisoners of War onboard. RAS(L)
> with RFA TIDESPRING, flying operations and
> "vertical replenishment" (Vertrep) by
> helicopter. Anchor overnight, armed guards
> closed up. (Wind SE, F3, SS3, Miles
> steamed: 140)
> We receive orders to "Proceed to TEZ (Total
> Exclusion Zone around the Falklands) with
> ANTELOPE".

NOT THE LEAST bit surprisingly, we had been ordered to continue south after the shortest of stop-overs at Ascension. HMS *Antelope*, in company with RFA *Tidespring*, arrived after dark on 12th May bringing prisoners of war from the recaptured South Georgia to be landed for transfer ashore. We turned over duties of Guardship to HMS *Dunbarton Castle* and sailed in company with HMS *Antelope* who was sailing south for the second time. Being of the same class, it was particularly helpful to be with another ship and be able to exercise and interact between the two. In particular, *Ambuscade* had somehow been left off the distribution of many of the signals and war orders that were accumulating in ever thickening numbers. Because we were gradually slipping ever southwards, first as Guardship to Gibraltar, then Ascension, it seemed the Fleet Headquarters were never really switched on to the fact that we needed all the information held by the rest of the Task Group. Not only could our Captain and Operations Officer get transferred across to *Antelope* to be briefed more fully, but we could exchange our officers and expert senior ratings to train up the other ship in exercises such as for Damage Control.

13th May
> 0615 Flying Stations for vertreping stores to HMS ONYX. 0700 recovered our helo, carrying out check test flight but second engine (of 2) failed on land-on! 0850 weigh anchor and sail in company with HMS ANTELOPE for Falklands, 1130 Vertrep, 1215 Flying, 1640 RAS(L) from RFA TIDESPRING. Speed 18 knots. Overnight, south westerly passage, speed 19 knots, ship fully darkened. (Wind south easterly, Force 4, Sea State 3. Miles steamed: 185)

Westbourne, West Sussex.   *Thursday, 13th May, 1982*

Good morning, my most beloved! Felt I had to start this letter while bubbling with good humour – letters this morning from various people, including my godson (now at Gordonstoun) and his mother, with a super outfit for the new baby – so exciting! – and, best of all, from you! The sun is shining and we are off out for the day, so I shall finish this evening, but I feel so happy to have heard from you and I wish I could demonstrate my love in a more positive and practical way. I worry about Alfonso's sex life – how is he going to learn??

Later – We have been to Portsmouth, had the exhaust mended

(it was only the seal round the top – they did it 'for the price of a drink' – so I gave them 50p. Lemonade??), we've had lunch out, and we bought a Large Box of fish fingers at Havant Hypermarket just to please you. I also bought a pair of brown leather sandals (phenomenally cheap!) on the strength of the non-bill on the exhaust. And here is a pair of throw-away sunspecs in case you need them, and a wee tube of cream to ease your sunburn. We have no jealousy – sun extremely hot here, and garden-watering necessary daily. There is an incipient purple flower on the magnolia! First batch of lettuces nearly ready, and flowers on some of the raspberries; potatoes growing fast and <u>all</u> the roses are alive.

News item: Barclays are to open on Saturdays.

Another news item: AW is absolutely sick at having to footle about in London instead of Doing his Bit – Nicola met him at a wedding last Saturday. The TV crews cornered the bridegroom as he came down the Guard of Honour to ask him and her what it felt like to get married 48 hours before going to war. He stiffened his upper lip and said, "It's what the taxpayer pays us for", and she said, "Well, how would <u>you</u> feel?" She obviously wanted to kick them in the teeth, and I don't blame her!

We picnicked with some others yesterday; Bim came to tea today; we go to a birthday tomorrow; bods to lunch on Saturday, and another birthday on Sunday. It's all terribly exciting for Alfonso, but he is thriving on it and growing fat on milk and salads and vitamin pills and <u>lovely</u> bronze eggs with rich yellow yolks which I am getting from a mother at school. She has her own hens, her husband is away, and she doesn't like them much, so I pay 70p a dozen and love it. I hope her husband is away when you get back! You would love these eggs.

There seems to be a wee rift between our Foreign Secretary and Thatcher – he is more ready to negotiate over sovereignty than she is – so you may yet find yourself in the front line. It seems *Brilliant* and *Broadsword* are taking it in turns to patrol the channel between the islands – wives are not happy. I've heard that some people suspect others of cracking up!

Must away to bed. I do love you so very very much, and I adore writing to you as the next best thing to talking to you. Louisa said this morning, "Are you happy because you've had a letter from Daddy?" "Yes" – "Is it like having Daddy here?" – and the answer is again Yes. It just brings your presence very much onto the breakfast table, and I do get tired of my monologue of endless trivia and meals out! Big big kisses.

Friday morning

Magimix insurance money came this morning, – hipra! Also a note from income tax asking for confirmation that our mortgage has gone up, which I shall do – present allowance is £1,566, which seems a heck of a lot! And I am spoilt for cheering-up letters from others! Long for the next one from you. Do you want copies of papers which I am keeping? All my love, my most adored man. Keep well, J xxxxxxxxxxxxx

14TH May

> Passage south at 19 knots. Engine change for helicopter. (Wind south easterly, Force 4. Sea State 3. Miles steamed: 451) Close up Defence Watches (for next 52 days).

15th May

> 0750-0830 exercise Action Stations. Check Test Flight helicopter. Anti-submarine exercise in company with HMS ANTELOPE. (SE F4, SS 2/3. 403 miles). Port Tyne main engine fails. Reduce speed to 14 knots to remain above 40% fuel level, in view of bad weather ahead.

BOOZE

Alcohol at sea is something to be taken in moderation, if at all. It so happened when I joined *Ambuscade* that it was a 'dry ship' on a voluntary basis, in that the practice was to take no alcohol at sea. (Officially the ration was for four cans of beer each day for ratings, with a slightly more liberal regime for the more senior personnel.) While I accepted this dry custom at first, I noticed that normal wardroom interaction was sadly lacking, in that the hard-working officers would leap in to the mess to grab a quick bite to eat, often by themselves, and then dash off to continue their tasks. The lack of communication and the impact on morale became noticeable, so after a week or so I told the Captain I was going to have a drink that evening and start getting the officers to sit down to an evening meal together. While he appeared none too happy with the idea, it was my Wardroom (RN custom is that the XO is the Mess President, and the Captain can only enter the Wardroom as a guest – an excellent custom that I have always appreciated, even as the Captain!).

So one Saturday night I went in to the Wardroom before dinner, stepped across to the bar and poured myself a half pint. There was stunned silence from those around me – until a Sub Lieutenant, who had earlier in his career been a senior rating, said, "Thank f.... for that!", and came and drew a half himself. From that time on, we met for a brief period before dinner whenever possible and then sat down together to eat, when not on watch. Morale climbed and other messes emulated our example.

My memory, however, is of a beer that had been left so long that it was pure vinegar by the time I pulled it that first night. It was only a sense of honour that made me finish it.

HMS Ambuscade.   *15th May*

My darlingest wife J,

Saturday night at sea – I even have had a ½ pt of beer – the first and last this week. Now 2300. Days start at 0600 or before and run non-stop to midnight or 0200 or so. But they are likely to get longer and busier soon. Never know, I might lose some weight. We'll have to cut down on food soon; no bad thing for it's been very good! Morale is generally very good and all goes well.

Had to sack one of my senior ratings – an important one with specific responsibilities under me. He was a walking disaster area. Took a lot of time to do and haven't been able to land him so could only warn him that we would demote him from Petty Officer to Leading Seaman. Messy and not wanted at this time. A shame, but no matter. Sea calm so far, but probably will start changing soon!

Sunday night

2330 and it was meant to be a relaxing day. Started again at 6 and this is the first time I've sat down, apart from quick meals. What busy people we are. Had a service again this morning – good attendance all of a sudden…! I read the lesson (Ps 23) last week and prayers this week. The prayers for our families are always the most moving.

We go around in funny dress all day – the blue shirts and cotton trousers are meant to be the rig, but I have to wear overalls (white). We carry lifejackets and bandages, and the officers morphine – all slung on a belt to which we will add survival suits tomorrow – equipped for anything! BBC World News is our update so you know as much as we do. Some stores and a little mail (some 6 letters only – not from you!) splashed into the sea today, but most of our mail would appear to be elsewhere. Can only think that this will reach you once we are flying our aircraft out of the F.I.

Darling one, I love you, long for you, and will be with you as soon as possible. In the meantime, be brave – look after everyone, including Alfonso, and especially yourself. You are everything to me! All my love, J

HMS Ambuscade.   *15th May*

Hello Louisa and Marc, I am writing this quickly as we expect to send it away in a helicopter in 5 minutes. The helicopter will take it to another ship, which will then send it on to yet another which is heading homewards.

I am a very long way away and it's getting colder. It may even snow soon, which sounds funny when it's nice and sunny (I hope) with you. I hope you are having a lovely time – at school and at home. Look after Mummy, she's the most precious person in the world. You are the luckiest children alive. Lots and lots of love Daddy

16th May
    0130 Moonrise; ANTELOPE visible by
    moonlight at 7 miles. Airdrop by RAF
    Hercules aircraft, subsequent Vertrep. Bag
    of Classified Books lost overboard while
    being transferred, swimmer jumps in off
    ship to recover but gets into difficulties,
    Gemini launched to recover swimmer and bag.
    AMBUSCADE ordered to increase to 18 knots,
    the Fleet Command accepting that fuel will
    drop under 30%. Helicopter engine change.
    Evening Check Test Flight helo. (Winds
    variable Force 4, Sea State 2. 390 miles)

Westbourne, West Sussex.   *Sunday 16th May 1982*

Darling one, – hope this reaches you as a free letter! The enclosed tax form is unsigned, so get on wiv it, mate. I don't think anything else needs filling in, and I have already written to confirm the increase in our mortgage. By the way, I am right to continue with BFPO Ships – the other address is for The Troops.

This was the news in a special supplement to *Navy News*

which plopped through the door yesterday – it's a Task Force Families Non-News Chummy thing, and I hated getting it because it confirmed to me that you really are part of the whole thing. I have been trying to kid myself that you didn't really belong to the chaps who were properly involved – but at least I no longer feel guilty about all the sympathy coming my way! I need it all – plus a bit of practical help with the mower, which goes click-click-click before deciding to run, and which cuts out every three minutes. Steve conveniently rang last night to cheer me up, which I much appreciated despite it being mid-story time – he suggests something caught in the blades, but I can't see anything. Anyway, I have managed to mow the New Grass and it all looks smart.

First Runner Bean up, peas looking good, the sweet corn all planted out, French beans plopping up daily, artichokes and sprouting and leeks all hardened off ready for planting out, all clematis doing well, two dahlias peeping through, broad beans as big as a pencil, apple blossom all set and snowing down, one nastily purple (!) flower on the magnolia, several tiny buds on the peonies, plum suckers <u>everywhere</u>, and my fingernails black and broken. All we poor deserted wives agreed at a birthday party on Thursday that the worst bit of absent men was having to water the garden all by ourselves! It has been amazingly hot and lovely, though it clouded over yesterday and threatened to rain after I had spent all morning getting a delicious lunch for various people including your mother. I really cleared up and did the flowers and exhausted myself and found your tax form – and it was all worth it because everything looked really nice, and I feel I can cope brilliantly. (But I shall go to bed early tonight!)

Today we walked up to the Common for a slide and Alfonso's first swing. He loved it! We lost Toad for two hours, which was the object of the exercise – it was the nicest way I could think of to give her a really good time, as she has had dreadfully curtailed walks this week due to our social programme. This continued today with Harriet's birthday – I made her a box cradle for her boy Clothkit doll which I knew she was getting, and it was a huge success. So was the party – all very pleasant and sunny chatting to friends.

Must go and make Wee's school dress. I do miss you so horribly and love you so much. Please God let it be over soon! Dearest one……..Jxxxxxxxxxx

17TH May
    0834 Sunrise. Helo transfers with ANTELOPE. Major Damage Control Exercise. 1902 Sunset. Overnight Surface Action exercise. (Variable winds, F2, SS4, 433 miles)

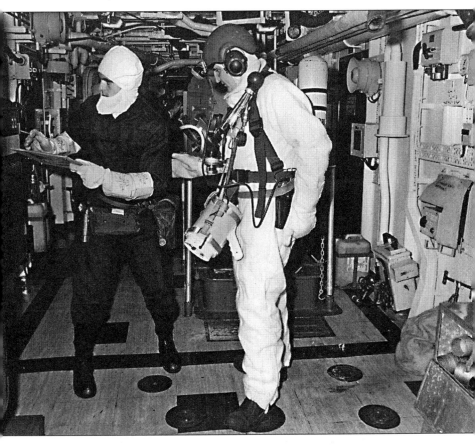

Damage control exercise. A firefighter is briefed before action.   **67**

BLUE MOVIES

One quaint little interlude illustrates some of the conflicting tensions onboard. By way of an evening's entertainment for all, a very old custom of the navy was to show movies at sea in the various mess decks. Films were dispatched by the Royal Naval Film Corporation (set up by Lord Mountbatten a generation before) to be shown in the Fleet. They came on big, old fashioned reels, encased in steel boxes and would be transferred from ship to ship at every opportunity. Film evenings were popular events that created good communal spirit. For instance, the Wardroom would traditionally show a Sunday Night Movie, and all officers not on watch would sit down to have dinner together and then watch a feature film, probably with a Tom and Jerry cartoon first. The banter was all part of the entertainment. The films were shown on an old-fashioned projector and the reels had to be changed a few times during the performance; the screen was hung from the deckhead. With a varying degree of success, we tried to show movies from time to time during the Operation for those off watch. The screen swinging wildly around in the rough weather and the projector tipping over just added to the atmosphere. We often never made it to the end because of going to Action Stations.

However, a new phenomenon was entering the Fleet in the 1980s – the close-circuit TV system. *Ambuscade* had one of the forerunners – a Betamax video machine, run centrally from a little office and cabled into each mess deck. Other ships had the rival, VHS system installed. While the reeled films still arrived, video cassettes were also being dispatched to the Fleet in the more modern format. Well-wishers in the UK caught onto this way of supporting the troops and started to send their own contributions.

Now it became apparent that certain men's magazines were sending complimentary films, blue movies, to the Fleet to bolster morale. *Ambuscade* appeared to be the only ship not receiving these, and eventually the reason became clear. We turned out to be the only ship still operating Betamax. The Captain was not disturbed by this, for he understandably disapproved of these movies anyway, but I knew the increasingly detrimental effect it was having on the morale of our ship's company. The Command was not looking after their interests. I persuaded the Captain, against his better judgement, to send a signal requesting some movies to be sent down in Betamax format, and some weeks later one arrived: 'Lady in Paris'. The deal I had struck with the Captain was that the Padre and I would check out the movie first to make sure it would be acceptable in standard. (I dare say we would have passed it anyway, or we would have been lynched!) We duly sat down in private with the Wardroom television set and watched. It turned out to be an utterly tedious video of ladies' lingerie, with five-minute stills of a bored-looking model and a description by an even more bored commentator. Not sure whether to be disappointed or relieved, we roared with laughter and passed it for general broadcast. To the best of my recollection we never had another murmur about the subject.

POSTSCRIPT

How times have changed in these 25 years. The reeled film has given way to video, which in turn has been largely replaced by DVD, and these can be viewed by any member of the ship's company on his or her own PC. The choice is now enormous, the thought of censorship impossible. But the 'film nights' for mess entertainment, such a companionable and morale-boosting event, is perhaps largely a matter of historical record.

18th May
    **0840–1120 Flying exercise (FLYEX). 0907
    Sunrise, 1800 fuel state 30%. 1918 Sunset.
    1930–2130 FLYEX. 2000, fuel state 29%.
    2255 Close up for Replenishment. (NW, F3,
    SS4, miles 359)**

HMS Ambuscade.   *18th May*

Jenny, my darlingest, We are going to try to get some more mail away this evening to a ship northward bound. Sent 2 earlier today. Now dusk, and we go in to replenish fuel in the small hours of the morning. We have to do it by a rather difficult method – so it will be pretty testing in pitch darkness. Oh well – such a shame my 'professional' seaman is a duffer and I have to rely upon others.

How goes things?? I hear from PM (who, lucky thing, received about 20% of ship's mail on Sunday – i.e. 2 letters) that you are joining up with other wives. Well done! Hope it goes well…

Darlingest, the situation is so extraordinary that it hardly bears comment. The snowball effect of the whole operation is amazing – who'd have thought this a couple of months ago! Let's hope and pray that it will be over quickly with the minimum of losses on both sides, and that we all get back quickly to our homes. Meanwhile, we've a lot to work to do and don't have any trouble sleeping! Do you? Has Marc stopped wandering in, or has he replaced me entirely?! Hopefully it's warm enough for you not to have to resort to your pyjamas. What a lovely thought! I'll be back as your personal hot water bottle before it gets cold again. Take the greatest care, dearest girl, and remember that I adore you for ever and beyond. J

Westbourne, West Sussex.   *Tuesday, 18th May, 1982*

My darling, darling man, It was such bliss to get a letter from you yesterday – and a couple of others to cheer me along. All very spoiling; but the best bit is to hear that you are still well and busy and enjoying it all. I hate to think that you may not see our wonderful garden this summer, but am resigning myself to a long lonely time, and pinning my hopes on your presence when Alfonso appears. I only hope he is a cheerful little bugger – you know how I believe in prenatal influences, and this has so far been a slightly tearful pregnancy! However, I am sure you will be relieved to hear that I am actually coping extraordinarily well, and I was told yesterday that I seemed the most balanced of the Falklands wives and least likely to crack up! (They're probably all told that, but still…) I have a little bump, but I can still disguise it, and there are a lot of people in Westbourne who Still Don't Know. I feel very pleased with this – 3½ months with no. 3 is usually impossible to hide. But I have these super big smooth titties all going to waste with no-one to stroke them – I miss you inordinately, and I just <u>cannot</u> bring myself to fancy the milkman!

The enclosed card is not because I believe in Fathers' Day, but because it seemed so appropriate! Marc was talking a lot about you yesterday – saying things like, "When I walk with Daddy I have to run". You are not forgotten! Two new things on the Marc front: I have stopped giving him a pee at night, and last night when he invaded me at 1.30 (which he doesn't by any means do every night, I'm glad to say!), I simply turned over and ignored him, and he eventually took himself back to bed and didn't return. A good new strategy!

The enclosed photographs I have grabbed from the albums will reflect my future state, I hope! J has said she will snap off a whole lot of us in our garden one day, so I will send those to you.

Talking of the garden, I have now planted out our marrows and courgettes and the three apologies for cucumber plants that I have managed to grow – plus 8 artichokes and our purple sprouting and leeks – and the sweet corn – and the tomato plants – this big! tomorrow. If it frosts we have had it, but I don't think it will. Still hot and sunny, but the odd rainy hour or so to help out. I have weed-killed the lawn and paths today, and I have got a Weed Preventer that kills seedlings – I can use it e.g. on the strawberries and raspberries and flower borders and anywhere that the plants are established. Such laziness!

Must iron Wee's new dress for tomorrow. She got a star for everything today!

My most beloved, do take care. Peace seems impossible, and I do love you more passionately than I can say. J xxxxxxxxx

View from the bridge.
Closing on tanker *British Esk* to pick up fuel hose.
Steaming down sea in force 10 storm.

CHAPTER 5

OUR FIRST
BIG CHALLENGE

S AILING SOUTH in company with our sister ship HMS *Antelope*, our course was set to rendezvous with a British merchantman, MV *British Esk*, which was a tanker that had been equipped to refuel other ships while underway at sea.

19th May
    0300 Heave to in Force 10 gale while tanker
    mends fuelling rig
    1130 Fuel state 25%. Commence ballasting
    fuel tanks.
    1445 Commence RAS(L), 1600 haul in
    refuelling hose, 1615 Start pumping, 1740
    Stop pumping, 1800 RAS complete. Receive
    and despatch mail to tanker. 2300 Commence
    cleaning fuel tanks. (ESE F10, SS9,miles
    208)

SIGNAL RECEIVED 191737Z:
    PERSONAL FROM COMMANDER IN CHIEF NAVAL
    HOME COMMAND.
    I AM SURE ALL IN THE TASK FORCE WOULD LIKE

TO KNOW HOW SPLENDIDLY THEIR FAMILIES ARE
FACING THE PRESENT SITUATION. THEY ARE
CHEERFUL, DETERMINED, HELPING EACH OTHER
AND ONE HUNDRED PERCENT BEHIND YOU. WE ARE
DOING ALL WE CAN TO HELP THEM. THEY WOULD
PARTICULARLY WISH ME TO SEND YOU THEIR
LOVE.

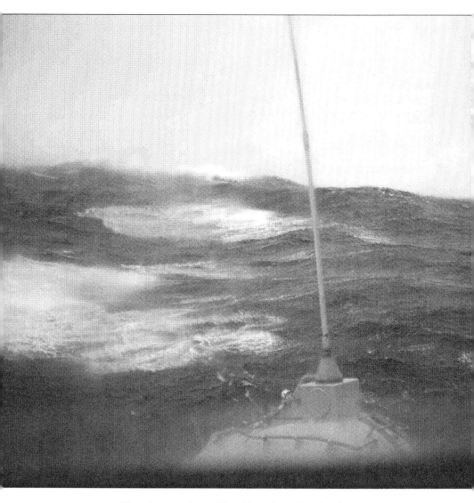

View from *Ambuscade*'s bridge of South Atlantic storm
while awaiting the vital replenishment. Huge wave
towering above us, some 45 feet high.

FROM DAILY ORDERS:

Lessons from the front:

As a result of HMS SHEFFIELD's experience and that of other ships in the Task Group the following strong recommendations will be implemented from 0800 this morning.

a) The ship will be in NBCD Condition Zulu at all times.

b) Doors are to be shut with all clips except 2 clips only on the main thoroughfare.

c) Anti-flash hoods are to be tucked into clothing.

d) In addition to lifejackets and survival suits, respirators are to be carried at all times. The respirator gives up to 90 seconds of protection in a smoke filled compartment and keeps smoke out of the eyes.

e) Parachutes are not required.

Declaration of Active Service

The principal effect of this declaration now made by the British Government is to place all civilian personnel in the Task Group under the regulations of the Naval Discipline Act. The additional powers of the NDA are only to be used where necessary for the operational efficiency of the fleet. At the same time the Commanding Officer's powers of summary punishment have been enhanced by doubling the maximum fine that he can award from 28 days' to 56 days' pay,

Beards
> So popular is the thought of discontinuing
> shaving that it has been decided to hold
> a beard growing competition. Rules will be
> published at a later date and judgement
> will take place on the return journey.
> This of course means that many more
> mirrors can be taken down and stowed. (We
> were picked up for them by NBCD Exercise
> umpires yesterday). Minimise mirrors.

The method of refuelling was for a tanker to stream a large hose astern of her which could then be picked up by the other vessel that had steamed up in her wake. The hose would be grappled some 150 feet astern of her, hauled onboard the receiving ship and connected by special fittings on the forecastle, forward of the gun and in the very eyes of the ship. That makes it sound easy, which it is not, even in calm weather!

As the First Lieutenant, I was responsible for the seamanship of such evolutions, while the Captain had the con of the ship to perform the exceptionally tight manoeuvring and station-keeping requirements for this evolution. There was the additional difficulty of sailing into a Force 8 to 10 gale with huge seas coming up unimpeded from the Antarctic.

Antelope went in first to replenish while we took up 'Lifeguard Station' astern of the two ships, ready to pick up any unfortunate sailor who might be washed overboard. For over twelve hours, while the three ships steamed on at 12 knots, *Antelope* strove valiantly to connect up and take on fuel. Despite all attempts, she was unable to pump the fuel across. Eventually her captain decided to abort the evolution and head off. She had enough fuel to reach the Falklands Task Group. It turned out that the hoses onboard the tanker had been incorrectly rigged and could not take any pressure, so they had to be recovered and the seals reconstructed. In the very rough sea state, this was a long and difficult task for the tanker crew. Indeed, the ship's log records that the weather during this period was a Force 10 storm with "phenomenal" (from the formal definition, see the end of this book) seas of over 45 foot high waves.

We did not have enough fuel to get to the Falklands so had to stay, in the increasingly desperate hope that the repairs would be effective. The replenishment (full title: Replenishment at Sea (Liquids) but known as RAS(L) or just RAS) was totally vital to our survival; we were several hundred miles from the next tanker.

Here I need to describe briefly our main engines and why we were different from *Antelope*. The Type 21s had the same engine configuration as the Type 42 *Sheffield* class: two Tyne gas turbine engines that were used for cruising up to speeds of about 18 knots, and then two larger Olympus gas turbines that were flashed up when higher speeds were required, giving a maximum speed of 30 knots (roughly 35 mph). The Tyne engines were economical, but the Olympus engines were very thirsty. We were sailing on one Tyne and one Olympus, as we had a defect on the other Tyne which rendered it unserviceable until it could be replaced.

Our fuel reserve had become low and the replenishment was essential, but the delay while *Antelope* attempted her RAS further exacerbated our critical situation. 29% of fuel was the minimum liquid loading required to keep the Type 21 stable according to the books, and there was a risk the ship could capsize below this figure. Other, more modern ships, had the ability to flood tanks to compensate for the fuel in order to maintain stability. In dire emergency we could flood our fuel tanks, but this would then make them unusable for taking fuel because of saltwater contamination and damage to the sensitive pumps. If we flooded any tanks we would reduce our operational range thereafter until the tanks were subsequently scrubbed clean by hand.

In the hours awaiting the RAS the Captain and Marine Engineer Officer, responsible for the stability of the ship, watched anxiously as the fuel gauges fell still further. We reached the critical 29% and held on, but then at 25% the command decision was taken to flood two tanks to help ease the situation.

Even then we remained on the margins of safety.

While *Antelope* had attempted her RAS at night, we were able to close the tanker in daylight, ploughing into icy seas that swept over the fifteen or so of us on our lifelines on the forecastle. For us there was no Lifeguard ship astern, for *Antelope* was pressing on ahead.

Good seamanship and no doubt a lot of good luck enabled us to connect the hose, after a terrific struggle, and pump the precious oil. Again, the ship's log records that this replenishment took very nearly four hours of manoeuvering close to the tanker in the continuing storm.

Everyone played their part in this drama, but the ultimate heroes were the stokers, who thereafter spent many hours in the fuel tanks that had been flooded with seawater and now had been pumped dry. They had to scrub the tanks out by hand to prepare them to take fuel again at the next RAS. It was one of the most unpleasant tasks to befall anyone in those rough seas, deep within the pounding ship.

Westbourne, West Sussex.   *Wednesday 19th May*

Darling darling one, Your free air letters came this morning, and everyone delighted except that Louisa would like a picture too, please! But I cannot stop weeping over the news. I had always suspected that you wouldn't stop at Ascension, but it is awfully hard to know that you are possibly in danger. The children are being sweet and comforting beyond belief, and they are such a help – but they only make me realise all the more how deeply and wonderfully I love you, and how desperately I wish you were safely at home with me. Pray God it won't be too long, but I have no real hope of this, and am expecting nothing. It all seems very hard, and I greatly look forward to meeting all the other wives and sharing the experience on Friday at the Post Office in Plymouth!!

We lunch with your mother today and leave Jerbs there until next Monday.

You will be glad to hear that I have arranged two breaks in the journey on the way back – lunch with my mother's goddaughter in Exeter; and tea to see baby MJ, born on 12th May. They are delighted, and A rang at 8.45 on 14th to tell us – an unseasonably early hour! We have presents organised for both Baby J and Baby F, who is due at this moment – rather fun.

I forgot to tell you that we had a call from Multi-Ownership – he swore it wasn't to remind us to pay, but to offer us another week at old prices. Our £3,400 villa is now being offered at £4,300 on resale – I feel that £900 is quite a reasonable capital appreciation over a month! I am wondering if Bim and I should take our fortnight anyway during school hols. – or perhaps we could have a week then and bank a week against your eventual return. Wales in mid-December???

This is all being written before nine o'clock, instead of my usual piano practice at this hour. I have found a new piece which involves me crossing over my hands, and the children love watching me play it!

We shall keep writing – Having heard that you would receive mail only every 10 days to a fortnight, I was only writing about twice a week. However, I'll get the free air letters and keep pushing them off, and hope hope hope that I continue to receive letters from you. I have been spoilt recently – but I deserve it! Oh, my beloved one, I can't ever tell you what you mean to me.

Come back safely. I love you. Jxxxxxxxxxxxx

20th May

    0750 Action Stations. 1000–1200 Flying
    operations. 1315–1500 RAS(L) with RFA
    PLUMLEAF. 1445–1700 Flying, exercise
    Crash-on-deck, . Stream torpedo decoy,
    1820 Gunnery firings, 1915–2200 Flying.
    Sunset 1932. All radars and radios silent.
    Ship fully darkened with navigation lights
    turned off. HMS EXETER approaching from

Helicopter secured on deck,
rotor blades folded, in South Atlantic seas.

astern and gradually overtaking us. (Wind
Easterly, force 7, Sea State 7, decreasing
5. Miles steamed 454)

FROM DAILY ORDERS:
RAS Yesterday Well done all those involved
in yesterday's RAS(L). It was a difficult
evolution that was carried out in a first
class manner. The following signal was
sent by MV BRITISH ESK: "Congratulations
on such a fine approach and RAS team
effort in such conditions. Sorry the milk
was late, you make our puny effort seem
very worthwhile."

Westbourne, West Sussex.   *Thursday, 20th May, 1982*

My most darling one, We are safely in Plymouth after a wonderfully uneventful journey. I collected Wee at 12.30 – got away at 12.45 – and was here by 5.45. Marc slept the first two hours and Louisa the fourth, so there was almost no time for bickering! But the penalty is sitting beside them now waiting for them to go to sleep – it will certainly take longer than writing this letter!

I listened on the way down to the latest debate on the Falklands in Parliament. It is obvious that negotiations have failed entirely, and we are waiting every minute for news of the invasion. L is in a stew, and only enjoys the company of other Falklands wives – so it's lucky that we can fret together! I may say she hasn't actually lost any weight over it...

As nothing has happened of great moment since I wrote yesterday, I shall try to think of all the snippets of news that I always forget. Like Marc and me finding a slowworm in our path while walking in Stansted – lovely demonstration of a Real Live Snake – and seeing two deer bound across our path and play in the field by the local woods with no idea we were there. I had my hair cut today while Susan looked after Marc – a great success all round, as I like my hair (which is slightly straighter!) and Susan and Marc obviously enjoyed each other's company.

I have favoured Prince Charles with a letter to tell him where his erstwhile chums are, as I thought he would be interested when you all start deeds of derring-do. I have also <u>brilliantly</u> remembered to get a duplicate car insurance certificate and organise an MOT so that we can tax the car in 10 days' time.

Now what have you done?? I long to hear every detail, and do so resent having no idea. I often wonder what you are up to, and trust that you are safely tied on when on the deck. Darling one, you are so <u>very</u> precious to me, and quite irreplaceable. I love you
Jxxx

These forms are inadequate! More kisses x x x x x x x x x x x x x x x x x

CHAPTER 6

JOINING
THE TASK GROUP

W HEN WE ARRIVED at the Falklands, the naval force was split into two main groups. The Carrier Battle Group (CBG) centred on the two aircraft carriers HMS *Hermes* (the Flagship, carrying Rear Admiral Sandy Woodward and his staff), and HMS *Invincible*. With them was a disparate group of tankers, ammunition ships and converted Merchantmen (Ships Taken Up From Trade, known as STUFT!). They were all escorted by a ring of frigates and destroyers to give protection against the enemy submarines that were believed to be in the area, and also against air or missile attack.

To minimise the real threat of air attack, which was expected to be in the form of Argentine Super Etendard aircraft armed with the deadly Exocet missiles, the CBG was stationed to the east of the Falklands at furthest range from Argentina.

Close inshore, the Amphibious Group with the 40 Commando Royal Marines onboard HMS *Fearless*, and 2 Para in the *Norland* were closing in on San Carlos water between the two main islands of the Falklands. They were to be the first assault wave and would be followed by 45 Commando, split between RFA *Stromness* and HMS *Intrepid*. 3 Para was also embarked in the latter ship. 42 Commando was embarked in *Canberra*. Vital elements of support, many of them specialised in the Commando role, with artillery, logistics, helicopters, medical,

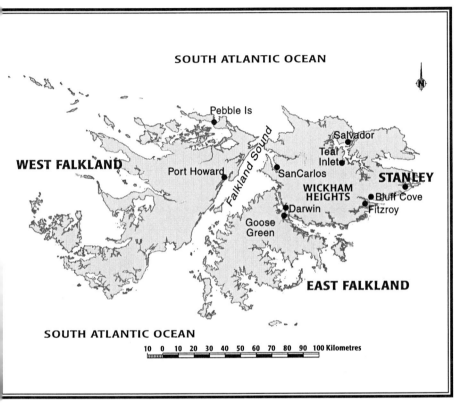

and missile defence, were embarked in 5 smaller landing ships and the North Sea ferry *Europic Ferry*. This large force was under the protection of 7 destroyers and frigates together with anti-submarine helicopters flying off the deck of RFA *Port Austin*. Sea Harriers from the aircraft carriers were essential in a role of providing air cover overhead.

We arrived with the CBG on 21st May, the day that the amphibious landing took place.

21st May
> **UK AMPHIBIOUS LANDING ON FALKLANDS**
> **1500 HMS AMBUSCADE R/V HMS EXETER in Total**
> **Exclusion Zone (TEZ) around the Falkland**
> **Islands. 1830-2010 Helo transfers; Captain**
> **and Operations Officer visit EXETER for**
> **Operations briefing and to receive full set**
> **of written orders from Fleet Commander.**
> **(NE then SW Force 8, Sea State 8**
> **decreasing 5. Miles steamed: 497)**
>
> **In Plymouth, UK, Post Office launch**
> **postcard featuring a mail delivery to HMS**
> **AMBUSCADE.**

The story of the assault has been told many times elsewhere by others who participated in it at first hand. The many days of meticulous preparation and planning paid off well. Diversionary operations had been taking place at different locations on both East and West Falkland islands, and the special forces had been well occupied on their reconnaissance missions and raids. The Argentines did not expect to be attacked from San Carlos waters, an inlet into East Falkland off Falkland Sound, which itself was the major passage between the two islands. They had expected the attack to come closer to the capital, Stanley, on the eastern end of the island, and they had prepared their defences ashore and with minefields off the coast in those more obvious locations. There was the real threat of air attack on the approaching amphibious force, especially as it went into the confined waters within the Sound, so a covert approach was required. At the same time, overnight, a party of Special Forces landed and captured the small enemy garrison on Fanning Head that was guarding the area. The landing commenced in the early

Action Stations on the bridge.

hours of the morning with 2 Para and 40 Commando landing in San Carlos and 45 Commando landing across the water to the west at Ajax Bay, followed by 3 Para at Port San Carlos. 42 Commando also landed there later that day. The troops had disembarked from twelve large ships, both specialist amphibious ships and troop-carrying merchant ships, and these were escorted by six escorts, all but one being frigates. Remarkably, 3 Commando Brigade established itself ashore that morning successfully and without significant loss. The next task was to consolidate the force ashore, but there followed a series of particularly heavy air attacks during the day from Argentine aircraft. The landing forces became spectators to the battles that raged between aircraft and warships operating close off-shore. Thankfully the landing forces ashore and in the amphibious ships were left unscathed by these attacks, but it was a bloody battle for escorts and aircraft alike.

Ambuscade arrived with the main battle group as the landings were taking place, and we were only able to listen to the progress of the battle over the various war-fighting radio circuits. I was glued to the High Frequency Anti Air Warfare Co-ordination net, trying to follow the battle from well over a hundred miles away. It sounded just like the exercises we had been engaged in over the years before: set routines of reports, efficient and abbreviated orders, descriptions of enemy attacks and missile launches. I had heard it all before in the computerized shore trainers, in NATO exercises, and in sea training at FOST. There really seemed no difference. Except that you could hear the gunfire and the bombs exploding, and the whoosh of missiles being launched.

Normally callsigns were used to disguise the identity of ships. The voices on the various nets were those of the Warfare Officers and the specialist operators; it was highly unusual to hear a Commanding Officer transmit a message himself. So when I heard the unmistakeable voice of Commander Alan West, Captain of HMS *Ardent*, come on air it was remarkable, as was his message. As I remember it, it was stark in the extreme and the use of call signs was dropped:

"*Yarmouth*, this is *Ardent*. Come alongside me and take off my survivors, I am abandoning ship!"

Ardent was our sister ship. The First Lieutenant was a very close friend of mine living in our village with his wife and children, of the same age as ours. The war, the loss of life, the effect on our families back home... Inevitably rushed and jumbled thoughts poured through the mind, but there was no time to dwell on them because of our own business. It was some time before I knew that our friend had survived.

HMS Ambuscade.   *21st May*

To the most wonderful girl in the world.
My darling J, The crunch has come and it's all been happening today, as you will have heard. It's now 2300 and I'm about to

turn in, for we shall be refuelling during the night – not particularly nice in the pitch darkness and I haven't done it like that yet. We refuelled in a Force 10 the other day and it went very well. Have spent the last hour wandering round the ship, talking to all those up – half the ship's company is always on watch. Tomorrow we go to action stations for the whole of the daylight hours.

We have been listening to all that has been happening in the air battle on our radios. I can't say anything now, but I am very worried about AGL. By the time this reaches you, you will have heard the news. It's very sobering indeed, but we mustn't dwell on it. Have no idea at all of casualties taken... It's not surprising that we are taking losses for we are operating in difficult circumstances a long way from base. I find it pretty amazing to see what we have actually achieved so far.

When will it end? Who knows – but we all long for the day when we turn northwards and return to where we belong.

Until then we must all be brave and look to the future. Darling girl, I live for you and the relationship. Thank you for being my other half – we are not whole without each other. I have every intention of being back safely with you as soon as possible.

I got 2 Economists and your lovely letter the day before yesterday. Super to hear all and that Alfonso looks OK. Sorry about Tom, hope that he is better now. Take the greatest care and look after yourself till I get back.

All my love, which stretches to and beyond eternity J

HMS Ambuscade.   *21st May*

Darlings Louisa and Marc, A quick letter to tell you that I am growing a beard - only 2 days old, but it looks like one already - hope it doesn't turn white!

DAILY ORDERS FOR SATURDAY 22 MAY 82   21 May 1982

OOD   MIDSHIPMAN BEVERSTOCK
Sunrise 1121 Sunset 2000

0730 - 0830 BUMPER BREAKFAST
1000 APPROX ACTION STATIONS

NOTES

1. ACTION STATIONS
   a. It is expected that the ship will go to Action Stations at 1000
   and remain in this state until after dark. It could be anytime earlier,
   however, so be fully prepared.
   b. Securing. Today is the day that you reach perfection in securing
   for action. Take note of laundry arrangements described below.
   c. Messing. A bumper breakfast will be served, followed by "Action
   Quarters Messing" and "Main Meal Action Messing" at various times of the
   day as the tactical situation permits. The system of Action Messing
   is fully described in Supply Memo 1/82 - make sure you read it.

2. RAS(L) We are expected to RAS(L) before joining the screen. Rig
   unknown. Those not wearing hard hats are to wear balaclavas rolled
up above the ears. We are at thirty minutes notice to RAS; this includes
   you going away to get changed so be prepared and be very quick.

3. Flight Deck Operations. For the duration of the Operation we must
   be at short notice to carry out flying operations. From now on it is
   taken that we are permanently prepared for flying in that:

   a. Gash will not be ditched - except when ordered by the OOW. This
   will normally be immediately after sunset, but may be more
   frequently if required.
   b. No Smoking is allowed on the upperdeck abaft the main mast.

   2 pipes may be made: "Hands to Flying Stations"
                     or "Standby HDS"

   Defence watch flight deck team are to close up if the Flight are off
   watch.

   Laundry From now until further notice laundry is not to be delivered
   to Sam on an individual basis. Messes are to use bags, clearly marked
   with the name of the mess, to deliver and collect dhoby. This is
   to be done on a 24 hour basis only.

5. Smoke. If the ship fills with smoke, after action damage, don't go
   back below to fetch your valuables or anything else.

                                    R J LIPPIETT
                                    Lieutenant Commander, RN
                                    Executive Officer

I have to sleep in my clothes at night, in case I have to jump out quickly to work. It's been very rough recently with big waves and white seas. Rather impressive but the ship moves around a lot. Still, I never feel seasick.

You will enjoy coming to sea in it one day, to see what I do. Looking forward to seeing you. Look after your precious Mummy. All my love, Daddy

22nd May
  0830 Join Carrier Battle Group (CBG),
  challenged by light and pass coded reply.
  0930 commence zig-zag. Action Stations.
  1045 Close up for RAS. 1245 collision with
  tanker, 1400-1530 RAS(L). 1600 helo CO to
  Flagship, HMS HERMES. 1700 fall out from
  Action Stations. 2000 sunset. 2220
  collision with HMS ALACRITY narrowly
  averted. Overnight screening carriers, 6-8
  miles from centre of force, altering
  course every 3 minutes.
  (Wind NW, Force 4, Sea State 4. Miles
  steamed: 407)

FROM DAILY ORDERS:
<u>Action stations</u>
a) It is expected that the ship will go to
   Action Stations at 1000 and remain in this
   state until after dark. It could be
   anytime earlier, so be prepared.
b) Securing. Today is the day you reach
   perfection in securing for action. Take
   note of laundry arrangements described
   below.
c) Messing. A bumper breakfast will be

```
    served, followed by "Action Quarters
    Messing" at various times of the day as
    the tactical situation permits.
RAS(L)
    We are expected to RAS(L) before joining
    the screen. Rig unknown. Those not wearing
    hard hats are to wear balaclavas rolled up
    above the ears. We are at 30 minutes to
    RAS; this includes you going away to get
    changed so be prepared and be very quick.
SMOKE
    If the ship fills with smoke, after action
    damage, don't go back below to fetch your
    valuables or anything else
```

Jenny's Viewpoint

It was a nice touch to invite the wives of the absent officers of *Ambuscade* to the launch of the postcard depicting the ship. The Post Office used to make occasional postcards, and this one was to show the breadth of their operations, with a Royal Mail van delivering to *Ambuscade* alongside in Plymouth. Going to the launch made a break, and it meant that I could see some of my friends in the Plymouth area. We had had a posting down there just after Marc was born.

It was on returning from the unusual party at the Post Office that I heard a lugubrious voice intoning the bad news: "Five of our ships have been damaged, two of them badly." I immediately decided that "badly" meant "sunk", and a cold frisson ran through me. I can remember thinking, "Keep driving safely. Get back to the house." When I arrived there, I was greeted with a panicky, "Have you heard the awful news?"

There were three beautiful whole plaice laid out on the kitchen table, waiting to be cooked for our supper. My hostess said, "Well, I don't suppose any of us is hungry now!", and put

Ambuscade wives in Plymouth at Post Office launch of postcard featuring mail delivery to ship. Sarah Mosse, wife of captain receives picture, while Jenny is immediately behind her left shoulder.

them back in the fridge. I watched her gloomily, as being pregnant made me need my food. Instead of anything to eat, we were given pint glasses of sherry to drink in front of the television. As I had completely gone off alcohol during my pregnancy, and disliked even its smell, I tiptoed back into the kitchen, poured my glass back into the bottle, and quietly boiled myself and the children an egg.

Later on, something made me say, "Our husbands are all right. I can feel it in my bones." I doubt very much if the other wives had any faith in this pronouncement, but they were comforted to a certain extent, and I myself felt convinced that it was true. I did, however, say that I was very worried about one of my great friends in Westbourne, as my instincts told me that one of the ships that had been sunk was *Ardent*. At noon the next day it was announced that Ardent had indeed been sunk, and I was not sure whether to be pleased or frightened by my prescience.

I had the same experience some days later, when there was a report that a Type 42 Destroyer had been sunk. I immediately said, "It's *Coventry*," – and indeed it was.

However, the good side of this was that I never felt deeply worried about John: I was (nearly!) always sure that he would come back to me in the end.

Plymouth   *22nd May, 1982*

My dearest one, All the awful news last night of the landing on the Falklands and the damage to 5 ships – I was telephoned last night to say that you were all safe, but life here is twitched beyond belief, and more than two days here would put me in a madhouse within a week! Supper last night consisted of our fingernails and sherry – neither very good for Alfonso, so I sneaked an egg and some salad while L and D adhered themselves to the TV and the telephone, which <u>never</u> stopped ringing!

We had a lovely Do at the GPO yesterday, and they say that a video of the events and copies of the postcard (which is well-composed, but even duller than I had imagined!) are being flown out to you. Pink champagne flowed all over the Post Office concourse, to the amazement of the general public – then we were given lunch in a rear room, and it all took so long that I got a fine for staying in excess of my paid-for time in the car park. Grrrr! Dearest one – off to Torpoint for a little fresh air with all the kids.

Love you <u>madly</u>, and am so relieved you are O.K. J x x x x x x x x x x x x

Plymouth   *Saturday, 22nd May, 1982*

My darlingest husband, This morning's letter was written in about 5 seconds and rather scrappy, I fear – Tonight I am waiting for the children to go to sleep, and I have more leisure to tell you ALL. I heard this morning that you hadn't actually arrived on the spot – due there this evening – so at least I haven't been fretting about you. The uncanny thing is that I told the others last night that the only fears I had in my bones were for *Ardent* – and I don't find my prescience at all comfortable to live with! I rang Westbourne tonight and gather that A is rumoured to be OK, but I wonder about M on *Broadsword*.

Now, on a different note, news, news. We <u>had</u> to get out today (being told last night, "Don't feel you have to stay"!!) so we lunched with S off a magnificent cold buffet and strawberries and cream and champagne to celebrate his engagement!. His fiancee is a viola player with the BBC Concert Orchestra – she is great fun and good with kids and S is absolutely dotty about her!! Isn't it marvellous? He is really quite expansive and has a huge 10 foot x 18 inches streamer up saying "I love you", and all inhibitions seem thrown to the wind. Wedding hopefully in August, but it depends on string quartets and <u>you</u>, as Steve says he hopes you will be his secretary in all this.

It was so nice to have something to celebrate – and there is also great happiness in the shape of baby C, who was born yesterday morning. The kids and I got back from S to find the others fretting away and no tea to be had – so we went to Millbrook to buy tea and to congratulate CF on his new son. They all seemed v. happy and blooming. We also popped in this morning to see BF, and discovered that, hip hip hooray, he is going to alternate with MW in the Ops. Room at Northwood, which gives me two super contacts in case I am utterly distraught over your fate at any time. In the meantime, I continue cheerfully irrelevant down here, and love you more and more. J x

COLLISION

Yet again, on arrival with the Carrier Battle Group, we needed to take on fuel, so we were sent straight in to go alongside one of the Royal Fleet Auxiliaries. These are specially designed tankers with derricks on their upper decks which can be lowered to pass fuel hoses across to the warship. The warship has to steam close alongside (around 30 metres off) on a parallel course. The ships

View from the tanker: the replenishment team on the frigate's forecastle, heaving across a line. Note the rough seas and wave up to deck level.

normally steam at 12 knots. Now this is an evolution that warships perform very frequently during their operations and exercises, and it is no big deal, even in relatively rough conditions. The Royal Navy is an ocean-going navy with huge experience of long-distance operations sustained in this way, a feature that was to prove a vital factor in our eventual success in the Falklands War.

However, although altering course while steaming close alongside each other is regularly practised, such alterations are carried out in small steps of 5 degrees alteration with a very careful procedure to ensure the two ships stay in the correct and safe station off each other.

When we joined the main body and closed to replenish, all ships were under Air Raid Warning Red (attack imminent), and we were at Action Stations. The Force was zig-zagging its course, all at the same time to the same pattern to maintain the fleet's stationing pattern. Alterations of course were every few minutes and of variable amounts, but up to 50 degrees or so. The pattern of changes was according to plans set out in classified books.

This was certainly a new situation, and not at all easy for the CO, who had to drive the frigate at speed alongside the tanker, which was frequently changing course. And because we were at Action Stations, the expert manning that was normally in place for any peacetime RAS was not always present.

The Captain drove *Ambuscade* alongside from his conning position on the starboard bridge wing, passing his orders via a microphone to the helmsman inside the bridge. It was rough, and there were strong winds that made the conning orders difficult to hear.

I had my team of some twenty on the forecastle, gathered around the gun, and I stood on the deck above and just astern of the gun to supervise the operation. Once alongside we managed to fire the gunline across and to haul the heavy rig on to our forecastle deck. We connected up the strong wire jackstay before joining the fuelling hose, some ten inches across in diameter, by screwing it into our special fitting. We started pumping.

The routine procedure, though in difficult conditions, was successfully completed when all of a sudden the gap between the ships started to close rapidly and a collision appeared imminent... I ordered the jackstay to be slipped and the forecastle to be cleared of all personnel. There was no time to disconnect the hose, for it would have been too dangerous. Our starboard bow hit the port side of the tanker and we were dropping back on her rather than maintaining our position abeam. The hose stretched to breaking point and then parted, spraying fuel oil around until the tanker could close the valves.

We scraped down the side of the tanker, making a frightening noise as the steel hulls ground together under huge pressure. We dropped astern to take up station behind her while assessing the damage. Thankfully no-one was badly injured, though I cracked a rib. Damage to the ship was superficial. We were able to regather our wits, and equipment, and return to the tanker within the hour, this time for a successful replenishment.

What had happened? My recollections may be hazy and I wasn't on the bridge, but as I understand it, the ship was on a southerly course with the helmsman steering, with difficulty in the very rough weather, a very precise course – say 164 degrees. The Captain on the bridge wing ordered, "Steer 1-6-5", to close, very slightly, the gap between the two ships. But with the noise of wind in the background the helmsman heard "Starboard 35", so he put the wheel hard over to starboard. When steaming at 30 metres apart at 12 knots, there is no time to recover from that error.

We were lucky to get away so lightly.

23th May
    HMS AMBUSCADE ON SCREEN OF CBG 0150 launch helo. 0335 submarine attack, launch torpedo, Action Stations. 0410 fall out from Action Stations 0510 recover helo. 1145 close range weapons firing exercise, 1540-1730 flying ops 1710-1730 Action Stations, sonar contact on possible submarine. 1845-2315 helo ops. 2300 large explosion and fireball observed to starboard (Sea Harrier crashing and exploding)
    (Wind W, Force 5/6, Sea State 4/5. Miles steamed 362)

TORPEDO ATTACK

Just as the rest of the ship's company worked watch on – watch off, so I alternated with the Captain in order that he should snatch a little sleep in the hoped-for quieter hours. The first night on the screen was memorable.

When in company with the Carrier Battle Group, we would be allocated a screening sector to patrol on the edge of the main body to provide protection from any attack. Let me just explain briefly what it means to be "screening". Escorts would be stationed at a distance from the centre of the force, with larger vessels such as the aircraft carriers, tankers and merchant vessels, in close proximity to that centre. One large ship would be the Guide for the whole force actually in the centre and all others would maintain station on that guide, which itself would be zig-zagging its course according to a set plan known to the whole force. The smaller escorts of destroyers and frigates would be allocated sectors to patrol, bounded by exact bearings from the guide and covering, say, 60 degrees of arc and at a range of, say, 6 to 8 miles. The exact area would vary according to the number of escorts and their individual war-fighting capabilities. In this way, the escorts would provide a ring of protection around the major vessels. The ship would then move around its allocated sector to cover the maximum area at speeds of two to four knots above the speed of the guide; the idea was to deter attack from submarines, using sonar, and to give cover from missile or air attack – and also to avoid colliding with one another. One key to patrolling the sector successfully was to carry out frequent alterations of course, typically at least every three minutes. This ensured the maximum coverage and also kept the ship from presenting an easy target to any submarine waiting to aim its torpedoes. In daylight hours, the station-keeping on the guide could usually be achieved by taking visual bearings of the guide, but in darkness with all ships fully darkened and very limited use of radars, patrolling the sector made considerable professional demands on the Officer of the Watch and called for skill, vigilance and steady nerves. For the ship's company, the frequent alterations of course, often in directions that were unsuitable for the prevailing rough sea conditions, just made life even more uncomfortable.

I had temporary command and was in the Operations Room, which was fully manned – as was the rest of the ship – to react to whatever came our way. The on-watch Warfare Officer was present to fight the ship, under my direction, and to instruct the Officer of the Watch, on the bridge above us, as to what course and speed to steer. The Operations Room is the heart of the warship at sea and had some 25 people manning it. The ships were all darkened with no lights showing, and zigzagging. It was in the Middle Watch, around three o'clock in the morning. "Torpedo, torpedo, torpedo!" the alarm klaxon sounded from the Sonar Control Room, "Torpedo bearing 185!"

Schooled to react instantly through years of training for such an incident, the Officer of the Watch increased speed and flung the ship onto a new course to counter the torpedo. Meantime the Principal Warfare Officer (always known as the PWO, pronounced PeaWo) launched straight into the counter attack by launching an anti-submarine torpedo down the bearing from which the threat was coming. Our reactions were instant and correct.

We had detected the torpedo on our passive sonar, designed specifically for this task. It could hear the fast-running propellers of the torpedo and give us a bearing of this noise. One could not tell what range it was at. We held our evasion course and went on tracking the bearing of the torpedo as it closed on us. A steady bearing would mean that it would hit us, but a moving bearing would mean it would pass us. As the noise of the propellers got louder, the bearing eventually changed and the noise then faded. We were safe.

We reported the attack to the flagship and carried out all the correct procedures to establish an approximate position for the submarine, and then proceeded to search for it. But after a short time we were called off and told to resume our station on the screen. Basically, the flagship did not believe us and said that this was likely to be a 'non-sub', perhaps a whale! To this day, the sonar operators, together with the sailors who were at their stations in the deep magazine at the bottom of the ship, swear that they heard the fast-revving propellers of a torpedo. I would love to know the truth, but the rest of the fleet put it down to "a newcomer's nervous over-reaction".

Incidentally, we went to Action Stations immediately we detected the attack, rousing the other 50% of the ship's company. They tumbled out of their bunks to close up, but the action was all but over by the time they arrived. Thereafter throughout the war we found ourselves going to Action Stations on numerous occasions throughout the 24-hour day to be ready for threats from both submarines and aircraft – threats both real or imaginary.

24th May
> 1045 Launch helo. 1135-1158 Action
> Stations for submarine threat. 1530-1700
> Flying ops, 1930-2200 RAS(L) by astern
> method. Overnight escort RFA TIDEPOOL into
> Amphibious Operating Area (AOA) in San
> Carlos waters and escort RFA SIR PERCIVAL
> and MV NORLAND back to CBG
> (Wind SW F4/6, SS4 miles 370)

HMS Ambuscade.   *24th May*

Darlingest one, It's 0545; I've been up since 0045 and have command (in a way) until 08. This is how we've been playing it, to ensure the Captain gets enough sleep. It's non-stop and time flies past – hard to find out what day it is. At the same time it seems like ages since we arrived. We find ourselves at Action Stations off and on day and night, with several scares and near-cardiac-arrests! We steam around as a heap of ships

H.M.S. AMBUSCADE   NIGHT ORDER BOOK

at Sea — ADA Escort Duty   Date 24th May 1982

PWO	1.	Escorting Tidepool to Pt Orchard and Sir
First		Perceval and Norland back to to Task group.
Morning		Carry out OPS' plan namely:
		a. Tidepool guide — Sp 17 (Granville), Co 275
		to pass through Pts Apple 3 and Orchard. PWO signal
OPS		PCS at each point. NC to remain in Apple Track
		b. R/V and collect Perceval and Norland as
OOW.		ordered by Plymouth. Running Co 090 Sp 12
First		or as necessary to pass through Apple 2 on time.
	2.	EMCON silent policy except sonar (ASW
		search and Station keeping), and occasional
Throttle		sweeps 16tb — detect minimum, 2 sweeps only, if
Today		sonar gives cause for concern.
	3.	Helo at Alert 15 from 0200 to aid search
Morning		if R/V goes awry or for other reasons.
	4.	Call me iaw CSOs and:
		a. For all important signals (PWO discretion)
		b. At 0230 or if the R/V time changes due
		to our SOA or Plymouth's.
		c. At 0800

JOHN CDR

Captain's Night Order Book for 24 May.

manoeuvring, avoiding each other in the pitch black (no lights, of course).

As ever, I can't comment on the battle for I know too much that is very highly classified. Listened to the news just now and hear the Argies admit that we have 600 troops ashore… And that their 30 aircraft attacked yesterday and all got back safely… How they can lie to this degree is staggering. I find the BBC to be accurate and often ahead of us in their reporting. But I am only too aware of the absolute agony it must be to you to hear that yet another frigate is severely damaged in the Sound and on fire with unknown casualties. Are you able to ring up the Advice Office to ask the name? You can't have any fingernails left by now – and is Alfonso OK under the strain?

I understand A has survived. How has home taken it all? Is Chris OK?… The most worrying thing of the whole business is the upset that it must be causing you. I can't tell you not to worry for I know you will. The only consolation is that our casualties are relatively light in comparison with the firepower we are up against. The overall military aim is being met (remember it ??????????) and therefore the strategy is working. Losses are bound to occur, and I don't expect to be one of them.

In these dangers we don't dwell on it and just get on with continuing to operate as best we can – I think that we are pretty efficient. My job is to go around spreading confidence and good cheer. Which I hope I do to you, my most wonderful wife. I love you. J

Westbourne, West Sussex.   *Monday, 24th May, 1982*

Hello, my darling one. I have just received a call from B to the effect that you are safe and out of danger. Could mean even that you are coming back, I suppose – but on the other hand, since they seem determined to abolish all Type 21s, I would have thought that they might have staked you out as a decoy to lure the Argentine air force (remnant) into the trap of Real Guns being safely operated from miles away by the rest of the Fleet. Funnily enough, I feel happier now that you are there, as it is a relief after waiting and wondering if you would get sent. And I have no nasty feelings in my bones at all (and remember, pregnant women are particularly astute at predicting things – fact!), though I did hold my breath for a minute when John Nott announced the crippling damage to HMS *Antelope*. Why do so many ship names begin with A, even not in the *Amazon* class. There are other letters in the alphabet – but I suppose the Navy hasn't got any further yet. (Oh, I forgot the *Broadsword* etc. lot – I suppose it's a step on the way).

We had a fine trip back from Plymouth. Saw Baby CF in hospital for a couple of minutes and they all seem very happy. Then on to Exeter for a rather health-food lentil-style lunch with the Ls and their 4 and 6-year-old daughters – all went very well, and we played on the swings and so on opposite their house before moving on to tea at Compton Chamberlayne. The baby is utterly adorable and very good, and they seem very happy. But I think A would rather like to join in the scrap at the Falklands!

We got home about 8, and the children both went miraculously to sleep while I had non-stop telephone calls. Someone had the bad taste to ring up during the critical part of the news – I am now like all our parents, and the news is sacrosanct! However, I do assure you that I am <u>not</u> like some of the other wives, who will be fingernail-less alcoholics by the time the Fleet returns. L even didn't go to her sister's wedding on Friday – she won't leave the house! I had to go out and buy tea and two litres of sherry on Saturday. The lady in the Naafi remembered me despite my hair-cut, and seemed very pleased to see us all again, which was nice.

I had better send love / regards or what-have-you from all those I saw – and those who phoned – and from those who wrote. I hope you feel better for it!

Westbourne, West Sussex.   **Tuesday 25th May**

The garden needs attention, but it is still rather wet. Yesterday I had to give a blood sample at the hospital, which took a lot of the morning, but I also retrieved Jerbs. I think your mother really enjoys having her, and apparently she behaved perfectly. Marc, on the other hand, was less than perfect while waiting for the doctor, saying in a loud voice: "Will the doctor look at <u>my</u> tummy? Will he look at my penis? Will he cut off my head?" Fortunately everyone thought he was cute, which his mother did not.

Bad news – the buggy was pinched from outside a shop in North Street; the bread bin is broken; the dustpan is in pieces after the vacuum cleaner fell on it; the gas bill is a staggering £80 which I shall query; the car is due a full service and MOT, and car tax. Money is going to be in short supply – again! But at least I picked up a £1 roll-top red breadbin at Broughton's – and also a £1 doll's push-chair in very good condition, and with a nice high handle suitable for either child. Extravagance will never be rooted out, it seems!

Dearest darling one, I think of you night and day, and realise all too clearly just how utterly vital and precious you are to me. Take every care – and come back safely. I do love you more than you can ever know, and miss you desperately. J xxxxxxxxx

AND THEN THERE WERE SIX

Ambuscade was to have gone straight into San Carlos Water the day after our arrival, but because we were the newcomer they held us back to get our bearings and sent in HMS *Antelope* instead, it being her return trip to the Falklands. It was a routine task, using gun-fire support for the troops onshore.

Like *Ardent* before her, she was relentlessly attacked by low-flying Argentine aircraft dropping bombs. As happened with other ships hit by bombs, not all exploded, as they were dropped by their very brave pilots at too low a height to activate the arming mechanism. One plane was flying so low that it hit *Antelope*'s mast, bending it over ninety degrees before the plane exploded. But another lodged a bomb onboard, requiring the ship to anchor two hours later in order to deal with the serious danger of an unexploded bomb.

Tragically, while a tiny team with the expertise required for such a delicate job were bravely tackling the bomb, it blew up. A major fire ensued and spread through the ship towards the magazine. The ship was abandoned and eventually, the following night, she exploded, broke in two and sank. The spectacular photographs of this have given long-lasting images of the war.

The Type 21 Club was now reduced to from eight to six in just three days. HMS *Amazon* was on other duties during the war, to her infinite frustration, but for sister ships HMS *Arrow*, *Avenger*, *Alacrity* and *Active*, together with us in *Ambuscade*, it was a sobering time.

It was apparent that the Type 21 frigates' anti-aircraft defence capability was not good enough, especially when being attacked from astern. This was something that the Argentine pilots caught onto very early in the action. In *Ambuscade*, we recognized this weakness and lashed five General Purpose Machine Guns (the ones purloined by the Flight in Ascension!) to the stanchions and guardrails down aft in order to add more firepower. In hindsight, the enemy's attacks on the escorts proved misguided, for the amphibious landings were achieved successfully and British forces managed to establish a foothold back on the Falklands. This was the first essential step of the land battle campaign and the loss of two escorts was deemed acceptable, whatever the tragic loss of life.

Many other warships, such as *Antrim*, *Argonaut*, *Brilliant* and *Broadsword* had been damaged by the bombing while operating inshore. There was an intensity of operations that could be compared to some of the intensive campaigns of World War

Two. Whatever the sophistication of some of the weapons and sensors, these first few days brought many deeds of heroism on both sides. In the Argentine airforce we recognised we had some formidable opponents. We were also very relieved to have some air cover from the Harriers flying off our two aircraft carriers.

CHAPTER 7

EXOCET ATTACK

25th May; ARGENTINA NATIONAL DAY
  0335 boat transfer to HMS PLYMOUTH, then
  escort 2 ships back from AOA. 1108 launch
  helo. 1126 sunrise, visibility reduced in
  fog. Frequent major changes of screening
  sectors for escorts as carriers search for
  clear visibility for their flying
  operations. Our helo is exchanged for a
  Sea Skua missile-carrying aircraft.
  1400-1930 flying ops. 1936 Detect missile
  attack, Action Stations.
  2005 Close MV ATLANTIC CONVEYOR to assist,
  2010 she abandons ship, 2033 seaboat in
  water searching for survivors, 2115
  searchlight search of water. 2150 fall out
  from Action Stations. 2217 leave ATLANTIC
  CONVEYOR burning fiercely and return to
  screen. (Wind SW, Force 5/6, Sea State 3,
  367 miles)

  HMS COVENTRY sunk by bombs off Pebble
  Island.

We had anticipated that the National Day of Argentina, 25th May, would be a bad day – but not that bad.

While *Ambuscade* was escorting the CBG some 60 miles north of Port Stanley, capital of the Falkland Islands, the hostile aircraft attacks were underway yet again. They were attacking positions where a number of our escorts were protecting the troops ashore. We followed the battles as best we could by listening to the fighting frequencies on the radios, and heard that HMS *Coventry* had been badly hit by bombs. She had managed to destroy two Argentine Skyhawk planes with her Sea Dart missiles, but another wave of Skyhawks hit her four times, and she capsized within a few minutes. Another major loss, though miraculously only 19 of the crew were killed, and another died later.

Our group of ships was formed up to give cover to the large container ship *Atlantic Conveyor*, which was heading for San Carlos Water with vital equipment to assist the troops ashore in their advance on the Argentine stronghold at Port Stanley. In particular, she carried troop-carrying Chinook and Wessex helicopters, and ammunition.

HMS *Invincible* and *Hermes* both had frigates close to them as 'goalkeepers', to defend them from missile attack, and *Atlantic Conveyor* was with them. *Ambuscade* and HMS *Glamorgan* were positioned further out, to be the first in line for the waves of enemy aircraft from Argentina.

1436: "FLASH FLASH FLASH. This is [*call sign Ambuscade*]. AGAVE Radar bearing 346 degrees."

Two enemy Super-Etendard aircraft, each armed with an air-to-surface Exocet sea-skimming missile, had approached the fleet at low level and then gone high to switch on their Agave radars to locate us. As soon as they did this, we first detected their radar transmissions and then saw the aircraft as contacts on our own radars. They were about 28 miles away (40 from *Hermes*), and they were coming directly for us.

1438 "FLASH. This is [*call sign Ambuscade*], Zippo based on Exocet missile release."

We had detected the launch of the missiles and the switching-on of the missiles' own radars. They were now 22 miles away from us.

A 'Zippo' is the reaction to exactly this type of attack. It is what we had practised in the years before as self-protection manoeuvres against enemy missiles, and we had been rehearsing our reactions with drills at least every watch ever since leaving Ascension Island. So we knew exactly what to do: what course and speed to steer in relation to the missile, and where to fire our decoys from both the 4.5" gun and the missile launchers. Known as 'chaff', these were clouds of aluminium foil that created radar echoes to fool the missiles' radars.

It went like clockwork with all those drills. While the Captain was in the Operations Room, fighting the ship, I was closed up on the bridge. We were at Action Stations with all our armament manned and ready. Damage Control Parties were fully prepared, and it was my job to keep the Ship's Company briefed on what was going on as I listened in to the radio circuit and the Warfare Officers.

The two aircraft had immediately turned away having launched their attack, but we held the Exocet missiles on our radars and electronic warfare sensors. We knew exactly where they were, and they were coming directly for us, at a phenomenally fast speed.

"2 missiles bearing Green 135, range 16 miles," I told the ship's company on the main broadcast.

"2 missiles bearing Green 135, range 14 miles."

"2 missiles bearing Green 135, range 10 miles."

And so they closed. As the relative bearing on our starboard quarter remained steady, it was apparent they were heading straight at us. We continued to fire our chaff and turned to the evasion course. One PWO, stationed on top of the bridge, reported that he could now see them both heading for us.

Our close-range weapons, the Oerlikon 20 mm guns and the

General Purpose Machine Guns, opened fire. This was a meaningless gesture in terms of likelihood of hitting a missile, in terms of both range and accuracy, for they were aimed by eye, but it was an excellent morale booster! And one of my enduring memories of the action at this point was to observe that Very Pistol flares continue to burn underwater after they have dropped out of the air... Who was firing Very flares, designed to burn red, green or white in the air for a minute or so to indicate a distress signal? It was our Padre. Being a Man of the Cloth, he was not allowed to take up arms. However he had decided that a flare was not a weapon, and that therefore it was permissible to fire them against attackers. We had already thought that it was a good wheeze to fire them against any manned aircraft approaching us, for it might put off the pilot at a crucial stage as he made his attack. But to fire a series of them against two missiles? It made no sense, but perhaps it was better to do something rather than nothing.

As I watched the flares burning as they hit the sea on our starboard beam, I was reporting: "2 missiles, Green 135, range 8 miles." and mentally preparing myself to fight the fires and damage after missile impact. At this moment the MV *Atlantic Conveyor* hove into view on our starboard quarter at a range of about 2 and a half miles. This was the area in which we had been laying our chaff decoys, and I immediately could see the danger – she was larger than any chaff cloud, and she was an obvious target should the missiles be decoyed.

The missile bearing was now starting to change. The missiles had been seduced by our chaff. We were saved, but, as they flew through the chaff, their radars started searching again and instantly found *Atlantic Conveyor*. She had turned away to present her stern as the smallest target and the strongest part of the superstructure. At 15.41, just 3 minutes after the missile launch, one missile flew into the ship some six feet above the waterline. In *Ambuscade* we swore we saw the second missile fly through the hole made by the first. While the warheads did not explode (similar, in this respect, to the attack on *Sheffield*), the

20mm Oerlikon firing.

missiles' motors continued to burn, setting fire to the ship and quickly turning it into a raging inferno.

Atlantic Conveyor was stopped dead in the water. Helicopters were attempting to rescue the crew, and *Ambuscade* and *Alacrity* closed her to assist. While *Ambuscade* gave cover, *Alacrity* went almost alongside her to assist the survivors, who had taken to the life rafts as they abandoned ship. The hull was glowing red hot from the fires within. Our sea boat, not designed for the rough, hostile waters, was lowered to search for men in the water. After dark and a final search for survivors using our searchlights, having found no further signs of life we left and continued our patrolling, leaving the deserted hulk afloat and on fire.

The loss of *Atlantic Conveyor* was devastating, both to us personally for having been so involved in the action, and to the British war effort, which was set back considerably by the loss of the equipment onboard. In *Ambuscade* we felt a very keen responsibility, having carried out all the correct drills but having then seen the conclusion of a ship being lost – especially one that had no defence itself. Nonetheless, we were pleased that we had provided the first warning of attack to the Fleet and that the subsequent actions had prevented the prime targets, the aircraft carriers, from being sunk

As I took charge of hoisting the seaboat, I stopped by the Oerlikon and picked up three empty cartridge cases – a memento for each of my children in the future of an extraordinary day in my life. I was alive but realised that there had been considerable casualties that day, the Argentine National Day.

We were despatched from the CBG the next day to go and find *Atlantic Conveyor* and see if she could be saved, if still afloat. We found her some sixty miles to the west, smouldering rather than burning. Launching our helicopter, we were intending to send a boarding party to recce the damage. As it closed to land onto the ship there was an explosion as ammunition blew up. Wisely retreating, we passed our report back to the flagship. A tug was despatched to take her in tow, but she sank before this was possible.

The hulk of *Atlantic Conveyor* still burning the day
after she was hit by Exocet Missiles.
She sank shortly after this photo was taken.

Some twelve men lost their lives in the *Atlantic Conveyor*, one
of them being the Captain, Ian North. He was posthumously
awarded the Distinguished Service Cross. Happily, none of the
other 43 British merchant ships serving with the Task Force
suffered serious damage.

HMS Ambuscade.   *25/5*

Dear Louisa and Marc, Another quick letter to tell you that I am alright, even if I am a long way away. You must have a look at a map to see where I am – perhaps Granny's globe would help.

I suppose that now you both go to school, Mummy just puts her feet up half the day and reads Country Life. Or is she scrubbing the floors, washing the car, doing the washing, weeding the garden, mowing the lawn (has the grass seed turned into grass yet?) and all the other chores that come her way? Look after her and help her as much as you can.

I think that some letters may reach us tomorrow, and I look forward to them. Do draw me a picture, both of you – perhaps you could draw me what is growing in the garden.

Is it nice and hot at home yet? Since arriving here, it's been quite fine, not too rough, and although there is a chill in the air it's not too bad. I've even got some long woolly knicks if it gets colder.

Look after yourselves – I'll be back to see you before too long. Lots of love from Daddy

HMS Ambuscade.   *26/5*

My darlingest J, Another letter, although I have no news. It looks as though we may get some mail away in a returning ship, perhaps tomorrow. Also we hope for some mail – arriving tomorrow... looking forward to it.

You mentioned good finances in your last letter. I think that May pay was put in the bank at the beginning of the month as we left Gibraltar. So don't get carried away, for I don't know when June's will appear!

We tick over here and are getting used to the somewhat different routine. Up a lot of the time. We refuelled from a tanker in the complete darkness last night – a bit hairy and very much my responsibility for the whole operation except for station keeping and ship handling – which of course is the Captain's.

I'll listen to the world news to hear what they say – then I'll know how much I can tell you of latest events…

23.30 Not mentioned, but I understand that yesterday they announced that *Antelope* had been sunk. As ever a bitter blow, but thankfully only 1 dead.

This evening has been one that I will remember for life. We came under missile attack at dusk. I can't tell you here, except that we, AMB, were exceptionally lucky and survived by good drills alone. Another (merchantman) was hit and is on fire and abandoned. You will have heard about it by the time you read this.

I must to bed as I'm on call all night. All my love to you my darlingest wife. I shall be back. J

26th May

> During night sonar contact, followed by helicopter attempting to drop depth charges. 1040 launch helo. 1131 sunrise. 1240 Action Stations Rendezvous in AOA with RFAs TIDEPOOL, FORT AUSTIN, STROMNESS, RESOURCE, SIR BEDEVERE to escort back to CBG. 1300 Detach to find ATLANTIC CONVEYOR hulk. 1330 launch helo to search for and then recce hulk. While half a mile short of landing onboard ATLANTIC CONVEYOR, large explosion onboard as ammunition blew up, but helo returns unscathed. Return to CBG, 2100-2330 RAS(L) from RFA OLMEDA. (Wind SW F5, SS3. 403 miles)
> Reinforcements arrive in TEZ from UK, led by HMS BRISTOL.

FROM DAILY ORDERS:

  <u>That was the day that was — and still is</u>
  The dusk attack on the force was first
  detected by Leading Seaman (EW) P. His
  correct and timely warning enabled the
  whole battle group to take what
  precautions they could.
  The vast number of drills carried out by
  AMBUSCADE'S team paid off. There is every
  indication that the missile would have hit
  us, had not the correct drills been
  carried out. Well done, all concerned.
  The firing of light weapons (including the
  Very Pistol!) would have frightened off
  the most heroic pilot. However, aspects of
  gunnery control must be investigated and
  our keen gunners will be under just a wee
  bit more control in future.

Westbourne, West Sussex.   *Wednesday, 26th May, 1982*

Darlingest one, How I hope you are All Right! The awful thing about so many ships going down is that there will be nothing left for you to command. I don't suppose they'd let you have a go in a submarine, would they??

It's been a glorious day and everything in the garden is growing magnificently, and it's impossible to imagine the cold and wet that you must be going through – and all without your woolly vest. Do you want a Red Cross parcel of Damart knicks?? All that I have heard is going out to you is a large parcel of books – and we all know how much time you have to put your feet up with a pipe and a novel…

Went to see J after going to watch Wee dancing. The news that the Super Etendards crept up from behind is disquieting – so look behind you <u>now!</u>

I decided to treat myself to a crab today – so many people have telephoned to tell me how I deserve everything – so I thought I would have a crab and mentally put some in your mouth too. It was somewhat spoilt by Louisa screaming in the house because I wouldn't let her bring a book outside – not the idyllic garden picnic I had envisaged – but we got over it. Tomorrow is her Sports Day – should be a guinea a minute, since it is non-competitive and no-one is allowed to win. We sit and drink picnic squash on the side lines and cheer – should be rather fun.

The neighbour handed a begonia through the fence today; the vicar came on a pastoral visit, and Mags rang this evening to see that all was well. Thomas merely has Acute Juvenile Rheumatism, and is now hobbling about – it's all much less worrying than rheumatic fever, so they are greatly relieved.

I long to get mail from you, but don't expect much. Darling, everyone is praying for you – God is on overtime – and I am loving you madly from a distance. How I long for your return – my darling one Jxxxx

CHAPTER 8

CHANGE OF
TEMPO

DESPITE THESE setbacks at sea, the land forces ashore
had started consolidating their hold, and were preparing
for their move to the east towards the capital Port Stanley.
This was the Argentine headquarters and their main garrison.
With the loss of the troop-carrying helicopters that went down in
Atlantic Conveyor, the troops were going to have to go on foot.

The shape of the war was changing, and our operations
turned towards a pattern that normally saw us operating close
inshore to land under cover of night, and returning to the main
naval force formed up to the east of the islands in the day time.
Our war fighting capabilities were ideal to the roles assigned to
us. We would frequently detach from the fleet of ships in the
CBG to escort one or two merchant ships into San Carlos Water,
where they would then transfer stores or troops to strengthen the
gathering momentum of assault. Having safely delivered these
ships it would be usual to escort out those who had finished
their business inshore and get them safely away before dawn
came, exposing us all to the threat of an air attack. It did not
always work that way, for on 8th June *Ambuscade* found herself
caught out close inshore in daylight while escorting the
merchantmen inshore.

In order to reduce our vulnerability in this position, we
devised a plan which involved the helicopter laying chaff to

produce contacts on radars. The helicopter flew away from the ship and laid deceptive patterns to simulate the formation of the ships that we were escorting. We hoped that if the enemy were there and searching for us they would be confused and, with luck, attack the wrong target. Thankfully, no enemy aircraft turned up that day. (Postscript: Some years later I was contacted by the then Flight Commander who, while on an exchange post in the USA, had read an interesting article in an American Armed Forces journal. It described how the CO of one of the Argentinean Sky Hawk squadrons had complained about being ordered, by the Army command on the Falklands, to attack a formation of ships. It was in the area where we had dropped our Chaff; the Argentines had obviously detected it and been diverted away from us. We had had a lucky call!)

27May
> **Patrolling screening sector. 1215–1230 Action Stations, false alarm. PM Helo ops. 1700–2055 Action Stations, possible Mirage attack, false alarm. Overnight detach to escort MV ELK and RFA TIDEPOOL into AOA. (Wind NW F5/6, SS4. 396 miles)**

HMS Ambuscade.   *27/5*

My darlingest J, 0500, and I've been up since 02, having had 2 hours sleep. Looking out in temp command. Thick fog, lots of ships around with no lights on and zig-zagging about …keeps one on one's toes, but we're on the edge of the fleet so not too bad!

Replenished (RAS – rep. at sea) fuel until 2300 last night. All in pitch dark – first time and went well. Certainly getting used to this evolution, which is somewhat hairy!

Yesterday was somewhat traumatic. *Coventry* was sunk and then, as I described, a container ship was abandoned. All pretty close. Luckily loss of life not too heavy in circumstances. A bitter blow, but it's amazing how everyone bounces back and gets on with the job. Have to really.

How long will it go on for? I thought it would be over in a few days after the landing, but... Who knows?

What news at home? Have people forgotten about us yet – are they looking at Wimbledon instead?

Most important of all – how are you? Are you looking after yourself and doing as little as possible, whilst keeping yourself fully occupied?! How is little Alfonso? Have you decided boy / girl yet? Is he /she lively? What are you reading about and what is he /she going to be?! Are the children well? How is Tom?! Your parents, my ma, etc. etc.

Hope to get a little mail tomorrow, via WB's ship. Should have come across today, but we steamed off for a little solo mission elsewhere.

All my love to you, as ever. J

28th May
```
   0720 R/V HMS PLYMOUTH AND MV ELK, escort
   latter from AOA to CBG. 1100-1430 Action
   Stations. 1130 Launch helo to lay Chaff
   barrier astern. 20mm Oerlikon gunners
   onboard open fire on our helo, mistakenly
   thinking it was enemy. They missed! Poor
   visibility (4nm). Pm helo ops. 1700 R/V
   with CBG.  1915 Steering gear failure.
   (Wind NW F8 gale, SS6. 372 miles)
```

HMS Ambuscade.   *28/5*

My darling, Life was full of excitements yesterday – several Action Stations and alarms but no active attacks (on us). We've been away on a mission and are at present steaming back and about to go to Action Stations at dawn (11.00 – can you believe it? –

we're working GMT here) to be ready for anything they throw at us whilst we are in range and alone.

Most exciting thing of yesterday was mail. Having been told there was lots onboard, I was somewhat upset to find none for me. Some couple of hours later I found one – hip hip hooray!! A letter of 13th, with sunglasses and baby lotion! Super for the way back! Meanwhile I'm in a string vest (issued!) for the first time today, as it's getting a bit more chilly and rough. Lovely to hear your news – albeit somewhat old. Yes, letters do bring us closer. I wonder how often you get mine. Probably they'll all come in a bunch and then not for ages. I like these forms for one can fill it up and post it just in case there's mail getting away. We send it across by helo whenever there's a chance and then it gets transferred to any ship going home.

Please keep news cuttings – I'll read them when I get back.

No sign of an end to all this, but at last they are on the offensive ashore. Our news comes as often from BEEB as from ashore. You may know more of what is going on than the Admiral.

Meanwhile I must go and do some work. Have just wandered around the ship chatting everyone up, and have temporary command whilst PM gets his head down till 10.30. He was up all night (no, I did 2100 – 0030) with the operation, so I got my head down and had a solid 6 hrs. sleep – unheard of in recent days!

Darlingest J. What a long way I am away, and what a different world I'm living in. We are keeping it all together and are longing to get back. Be brave, look after everyone, and mainly yourself! Lots of love to L+M+A+J, but all goes to you, personally! J

Westbourne, West Sussex.   *Friday 28th May*

My beloved one, Letters today, which I thought would be a great treat, but in fact it has just made me miserable! I just cannot see an end to this, and I fear that even if the Islands are retaken, you will not be able to return. I long with every part of me to see

Ambuscade sailing safely into Plymouth Sound, and to know that you won't have to go south again! The loss of four ships so far, though, may mean that you have to stay there longer, and return to patrol there even after immediate hostilities have cooled down. Both Nott and Thatcher say emphatically that there is no question of Argentina being given sovereignty – but that is the only way to stop this lunatic war, and in my opinion the islands are just not worth the price.

I went out to Funtington last night. Another couple had been invited, but only the wife was there as he had been called away for something to do with the Falklands. It was a lovely evening and they were so sweet to me – even offered me tea instead of coffee at the end of the meal! It certainly cheered up a wet day – it didn't actually rain over Wee's sports day, but it threatened to do so, and the ground was soaking wet. Otherwise it was quite fun just chatting to other parents.

I do wish everyone would stop telling me I look ravishing – it's all a bonus of being pregnant, and I hate to think that it's all being wasted without you to admire it! By the time you get back I shall either look like an elephant or have three children, and either way I shall not look glamorous!

The children are leaping all over me – we have been to play-school this morning and are now about to pack up and go to Ciren. when Bim arrives. Oh darling, I want you back so very much. I have the feeling more will happen this w/e and I dread it. You are the most perfect husband the world has ever known, and I love you so terribly, cruelly much. Why do you have to be there? J xxxxxxxxxx

29TH May
    0820-0950 attempt RAS abeam but abandon
    because of weather, 1000-1215 RAS(L)
    astern from RFA TIDESPRING. 1142 Sunrise.
    1710-1830 helo ops. 1947 Sunset. Detach on
    first Naval Gunfire Support mission in

company with **HMS GLAMORGAN** . Hatch in door
on gun turret stove-in by rough seas.
Temporary repairs. (Wind W, F5/6, SS5. 301
miles)

FROM DAILY ORDERS:

<u>Ultra Quiet State</u> The position of the
minefield off Cape Pembroke is known and we
shall not be going near it. Nevertheless,
it is prudent to take all precautions
against the mining threat. The ship will
go to the Ultra Quiet State at 2359.
Ship's Company are to be as quiet as
possible closing doors etc. Heads
[*Lavatories*] will be out of action for this
period except 0200-0215 and 0345-0400.

<u>Forward Damage Control Party</u> in the threat of
mining, will be closed up in the cabin
flat (above the waterline) from 0400.
Essential Damage Control equipment is to
be taken out and stowed in the Wardroom
pantry.

HMS Ambuscade.   *29/5*

Darlingest J, I'll start a letter now, 2330. V. busy day as ever.
Spent 4½ hours, mainly in darkness, this morning trying to
replenish fuel in v. poor conditions. It puts years on me each
time! Now dashing off at high speed on a 'mission' and will be
at Action Stations from 0230 onwards. So sleep comes rarely and
only by the hour or two.

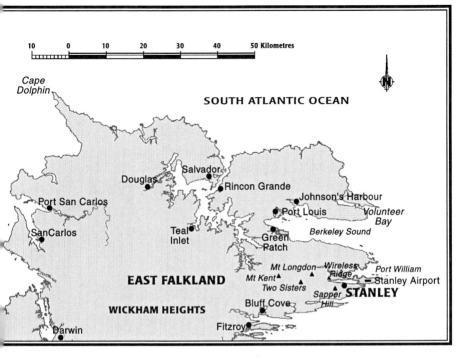

SHORE BOMBARDMENT

From 29th May onwards, *Ambuscade* was regularly engaged in using her 4½ inch gun to bombard enemy shore positions. Called Naval Gunfire Support (NGS), this was the main purpose of our gun, and one that had been well practised over the years before the war. The gun was highly accurate and could lay down rapid fire if required; 25 rounds per minute of high explosive could be highly effective. Type 21 frigates could even engage two targets at the same time, a smart feat for computers in those days! We were normally assisted by a 'spotter' who would report where the shells were landing and correct any inaccuracies of fire. The spotter could be the Observer in our helicopter, hovering over the action, or, more often the case in this war, would be army personnel reporting from ashore. Good radio communications were essential and we sometimes had an army liaison officer onboard to get optimum results.

The 4.5 inch gun. Fast passage in rough seas to close the islands for naval gunfire support.

On 29th May we steamed into the coastal region off the Eastern Island with HMS *Glamorgan* to lob shells into Port Stanley, but we later found ourselves inside the sounds and inlets laying down fire on Argentine troops directly in front of our advancing troops. The accuracy of our fire caused a considerable amount of favourable comment from our army colleagues.

On 7th June, in company with three other frigates, we entered Berkeley Sound inside the minefield laid by the Argentines to support a barrage of fire from our artillery and mortars ashore. That night we fired 228 rounds (about five tons in weight!) in support of the attacks on Mount Harriet, to the west of Port Stanley, which in the teeth of fierce opposition was being attacked by 2 Commando Brigade and 3 Parachute Regiment. The 9th June saw similar NGS in support of attacks on Mount Longdon and the Two Sisters. So confident in the accuracy of our fire were the troops ashore that they were directing our shells to land just yards ahead of their advance on Wireless Ridge, where they encountered specific resistance. Altogether *Ambuscade* fired

460 rounds, though our last foray of NGS was cut short by a mechanical defect that caused us to withdraw.

Two little incidents come to mind as I recall those long, dark nights of bombardment. The first time we went inshore to fire, the ship was at Action Stations and I was on the bridge to oversee the navigation and manoeuvring as we approached the shore line. We were steaming in, the ship fully darkened, and I was sitting in the Captain's chair. Our eyes were fully accustomed to the blackness, for the only lights on the bridge were the dimmed red lights of the compass and chart table. I was suddenly aware of rather ghostly white forms in the sea around us, and as I stared through my binoculars, I realised that these were plumes of water and spray

Setting off with two type 21 Frigates
for bombardment mission.

caused by gunfire (just as I had seen in prints of the Battle of Jutland – though smaller). We were under fire ourselves.

I then did something silly. In the darkness I got out of the chair at the front of the bridge and stood behind it. I suppose subconsciously I thought that if we were hit I might get some protection from it. Five seconds later I thought, "How daft you are, Lippiett", and went back to sit in it. If we were to be hit by a shell landing on the bridge, no chair was going to be protection! Needless to say, we weren't hit and our bombardment went on successfully.

Another memory of the bombardment also brings a smile to my face now. Mounted on the ship's superstructure just aft of the gun were various fittings, such as communications equipment. Included there was an alarm switch that would be activated if the ship came under Chemical Warfare (CW) attack. I cannot remember now whether the threat of this type of warfare was thought to be very high in this war – I doubt it – but we all carried our anti-gas respirators with us at all times in case we came under chemical attack. Like most military things, there was a set routine to be followed if coming under attack. If anyone detected an attack or if the CW alarm (a high-pitched Dee-Dah that sounded throughout the ship for some 30 seconds) went off, then you held your breath, put on your mask and yelled, "GAS! GAS! GAS!".

Unfortunately we had an intermittent defect on our CW alarm switch on the forecastle, and when the gun fired, the shock wave activated the alarm. While we tried to deactivate the alarm, we were not always successful, and there were not too infrequent occasions when we were all to be seen going around in gas masks while we had to confirm that we were not under chemical attack.

One night, the alarm just went on and on, Dee-Dah, Dee-Dah… I had been busy elsewhere in the ship but made my way to the Operations Room to see what was going on. Wrongly, I had removed my mask, knowing that the alarm had sounded as soon as we had fired the first round, and that this again was a false alarm. Entering the Ops Room I was rather surprised to see them all fully clad in their masks, desperately trying to fight the ship in the very difficult conditions of muffled communications through a mask. I reported to the Captain, who told me we thought we were indeed under gas attack. Well, either we were and I was doomed, or there was a tremendous muddle as to the authenticity of the alarm. We decided I was not dead, so off came the masks.

One further little anecdote. The soldier who had joined us that night for the bombardment to be the Liaison Officer was aghast to see everyone donning their masks and shouting, "GAS! GAS! GAS!". Not carrying a gas mask himself, he clutched some anti-flash gloves (made of cotton) to his nose and just hoped for the best. He was mightily relieved to see me walk into the Ops Room without a mask...

ANOTHER DAY – ANOTHER EXOCET!

30th May
> 0110 Test firing of 4.5 inch gun. 0315-0750 Action Stations. 0335 engaging Port Stanley and Fitzroy. 94 rounds. Under fire from shore batteries. 1138 Sunrise. Return to CBG. 1355 Vertrep ammunition from RFA FORT REGENT in difficult conditions in gale.
> 1730 Action Stations. Force under missile and aircraft attack. Exocet missile seen by Starboard 20mm gun crew, who open fire (range 7 miles, no chance!). Large explosion seen at Green 160.
> 1800 Launch helo to HMS AVENGER for covert insertion of SBS and spotters into Falklands. 1938 Sunset. Flight conduct radar blind pilotage up a dry river bed with no moon to land SBS, while AVENGER

fires 4.5" shells over the top to drown out rotor noise while they insert 6 loads of personnel. R/V with HMS BRILLIANT and RFA TIDEPOOL for passage to AOA. (Wind W, F4, SS 3/5. Miles 416)

Another call to Action Stations was more than real. *Ambuscade*, for the second time of the war, was the first ship to detect an Exocet attack on the main force. It closed the force, came under fire from our sister ship HMS *Avenger* (commanded by the Captain of the Fourth Frigate Squadron) and was reported as flying very close over the top of her flight deck. Their fire caused much concern to *Ambuscade's* helicopter crew who were at that very time hovering alongside and below the level of *Avenger's* flight deck. Whether or not the Exocet had been shot down or had just come to the end of its maximum range, it did no harm and turned out to be the last Exocet attack from the air in the war. But we were not to know that, and remained fully alert and expectant throughout, continuing to carry out the Chaff drills every watch.

*   *   *

And there lies another story. These drills were initiated by the on-watch Warfare Officer, who would, at a random time, suddenly declare to the Operations Room: "For Exercise, Zippo Three, based on Agave radar". Thereafter, set people had set drills; the Officer of the Watch would put the ship on the course and speed, the Flight Deck Officer would confirm the position of the helicopter (for its safety), and the Petty Officer Missileman would reach up to the Chaff firing panel above his head to do touch drills on the six buttons for the three launchers on either side of the bridge wings. Touch drills were just that, touching, but so carried away was the Petty Officer one night that 'touch' became 'press'.

WHOOSH went the missiles in their six salvoes. Red-faced, we had to admit to the Fleet the reason for six new radar contacts emanating from around us. Not for nothing was that Petty Officer known to all by his new nickname: 'Whoosh'. (My apologies to him for resurrecting this story – I owe him a beer!)

NIGHT HELICOPTER OPERATIONS

It was on this day and night that our helicopter became involved in a notable operation that I should now describe, as related by the Flight Commander. Special Forces (from both the Special Air Service, SAS, and the Special Boat Service, SBS) were operating on the Falkland Islands and naval forces were involved in their covert insertion and extraction. HMS *Avenger's* helicopter had damaged its tail rotor during a demanding night Special Forces landing, so *Ambuscade* was ordered by the Force Commander to deploy our aircraft to *Avenger* to support further insertions overnight of the 30th of May. As has just been mentioned, the aircraft arrived alongside *Avenger* in the middle of an air raid on the group and had a few hair-raising moments dodging the bullets from enthusiastic gunners who seemed to have difficulty spotting the difference between a Lynx helicopter and Exocet missiles. Once on board the task was briefed. It involved the insertion of a team of 20 members of the SBS and 4 Army Spotters to a location some miles inland. This would take place at night; the combination of overcast skies, no moon and nothing in the way of street or house lighting meant that this was going to require a high degree of skill. The Flight were not equipped with Night Vision Goggles as all of the units which had been air-dropped to us were made useless because of water ingress. The Captain offered to fire the 4.5 gun over the top of the aircraft as it transited in and out from the drop-off point so as to create a noisy diversion. The plan involved the use of the Lynx's high definition radar to home to a beach hut on a sand bar and attempt to use the radar to carry out blind pilotage up a dry river bed to a position miles inland which was the designated drop-off point. The aircraft was duly prepared and the aircraft cabin was stripped out to give the maximum amount of space. The 4 Sea Skua missiles fitted to the aircraft were taken off and stowed on camp beds as none of the normal stowage trolleys were available! The launch hour came and the 4.5 gun opened fire, the aircraft took off and transited at low speed about 20 feet above the sea. The sand bar, beach hut and dry river bed stood out well on radar and the Pilot and Observer set about the difficult task of flying at low level over unlit terrain following the twists and turns in the dry river bed until they arrived at the drop off point. The stick of 4 Marines and their spotter jumped out with their kit and the helicopter retraced its steps back to *Avenger*. Four more trips followed to get all the party and their kit ashore. Once back onboard, the helicopter was shut down to reload the missiles and replace the items removed from the cabin. *Avenger* made her way off shore and about 2 hours later the helicopter launched to face a transit of one hundred miles back to us for a welcoming cup of tea.

Westbourne, West Sussex.   *Sunday, 30th May, 1982*

My only beloved, I feel so annoyed that you haven't received any letters when I write virtually every day! Let's hope they haven't all been dumped in the sea somewhere – especially the pair of scissors I sent you so that your toenails will be in fine trim when you get back. I don't want scratched legs! But I do want you back soon soon soon, because Alfonso is starting to ask where babies come from, and I think a practical demonstration would be much the best idea.

We are spending Whitsun at Cirencester, and having a nice time with very good and adorable children. My mother has given each of them a child's folding garden chair and they are absolutely thrilled to bits with them. We had lunch with my mother's cousin yesterday, and Marc slept on her bed all through lunch, which was a tremendous relief! And we went shopping for a new dustpan and a breadbin, and got another Chopin secondhand record and a super learning-to-play-the-piano book for Wee at the music shops. Tomorrow we go to Doddington, a stately home near Bath with a railway and playground, so fun for all the family. The weather has been great – but I wish it would rain on all the bedding plants I have been putting in at home. A number of dahlias have failed to arrive, so I have bought some – also lobelia, salvias and bedding chrysanthemums. And I think I may have to buy some tomatoes, as every one I put in has disappeared – utterly vanished! I have some more in a seed tray, but they may suffer the same fate.

The Pope is in Britain and it's all marvellously ecumenical with joint services and much interchange and rapport between the Archbishop of Canterbury and the Pope. There was a joint service in Canterbury yesterday, and he is taking hundreds of masses and visiting thousands of people and places in his 4 days here. He is going to Argentina at the end of June.

News from the Front is encouraging to the warmongers, who are enjoying the vicarious prospect of winning a real battle – Darwin and Goose Green about to be taken – but *The Sunday Times* confirms all my fears as to what will happen afterwards. It will surely turn into a Northern Ireland situation – and if you are sent on Patrol down there, I am <u>instantly</u> going to buy us a farm. So there! I miss you somethink awful, and so long to see you home. Take every care, and remember that you are the most precious being in the world to me. J xxxxxxxx`

31st May
>   0107 R/V RFA SIR GALAHAD to escort out to CBG. 0655 recover helo. 1030-1220 Vertrep ammunition. 1141 Sunrise. 1245-1435 attempt to RAS(L), unable to because of defective rig. Return to screen as Electronic Warfare picket. 1800 detach for Naval Gunfire Support (NGS) 1938 Sunset. (Wind SW F6, SS5. 390 miles)

FROM DAILY ORDERS:
Bravo Zulu
a) Able Seaman (EW) S for being the first in
   the force to detect today's Super Etendard
   attack; UAA1 scores again!
   b) All those involved in the vertrep of
   AMMO. Conditions were far from perfect and
   you worked well as a team.

Small Arms Fire
   As was found in the first Exocet attack,
   the tenacity of those firing small arms
   against the incoming raid was superb. This
   is verified by our helicopter crew who
   nearly got hit. Control of small arms is
   difficult with the high noise factor. The
   routine in future will be as follows:
   PWO(A) MGD(V) will fire a very pistol from
   the GDP:

   GREEN: indicates the direction of the
   threat and gives permission to engage on
   that general bearing.
   RED: indicates check fire all round (Check
   Fire may also be given by 2 blasts on the
   siren)
   No one else is allowed to fire a Very
   pistol in this situation.

HMS Ambuscade.   *Mon 0100*

What a funny old day Saturday was. Sat/Sun night spent up and
v. busy. All Sunday pm spent ammunitioning in terrible weather.
Soaked to the skin – took 5 hours! Then more excitements –

another attack on us all – I can say this because it was on the world news an hour ago. Also on news that Stanley came under heavy bombardment on Sat night, so you can put 2 + 2 together to see why we wanted ammo yesterday!

Another mission tonight in progress, and so it goes on. I'm off to bed, exhausted. I love you. J

Still Mon 31

Back from that – no incidents. Prepared to take on ammo this morning on the forecastle in horrible weather in the dark; then they decided to fly it on instead. As soon as that was underway they decided we should refuel immediately after – off we went (missing lunch), 1½ hrs tied up to the tanker but failed to take fuel – their gear didn't work. So now we abandoned all, and are back doing our thing, with more 'excitements' through the night and no doubt two replenishments tomorrow. And so it goes on.

It's snowing now and pretty cold. Been on upper deck for 6 hours but have kept fairly dry this time. Could all change. Must finish this, lest mail closes.

Must sound dreadfully boring to you, but time passes in a flash. Have no idea what the long term prospects are, but hope to be with you as soon as they let us away. Take great care and write lots and lots of letters to me. All my love you. J

HMS Ambuscade.   *31/5*

Hello, Little ones, How are you? I thought I would write to tell you that it is snowing down here – how different to your summer – but then I'm at the other end of the world (doesn't seem like it!)

Next time I'll draw you a picture of my ship, and what is inside it.

What about you both drawing a picture for me?

Look after Mummy and make sure she behaves herself. Have

2/5

Hello Little ones,

How are you? I thought I would write to tell you that it is snowing down here — how different to your summer — but then I'm at the other end of the world (doesn't it seem like it?!)

Next time I'll draw you a picture of my ship, and what is inside it.

What about you both drawing a picture for me?

Look after mummy + make sure she be haves herself. Have lots of fun + see you before too long.

Lots of love   Daddy.

beard is getting
a bit longer now
9 days old.

lots of fun, and I'll see you before too long. Lots of love, Daddy
Beard is getting a bit longer now – 9 days old.

Westbourne, West Sussex.   *31st May, 1982*

Darling one, May Bank Holiday and the sun has actually shone!
We have had a lovely day at Doddington, near Bath – a rather
short house tour, an excellent carriage museum and a ride in a
horse-drawn trap, an adventure playground and a train to ride
around (twice!) and ice-creams and treats galore. All a very
pleasing day except that the children fell asleep on the way back
and now they won't go to sleep in time for me and Ma to go to
the film 'Chariots of Fire' in Cirencester! It's supposed to be v
good.

News from your way sounds reassuring – Goose Green and Darwin taken, and hundreds of prisoners rather than hundreds of dead. But there has been so little news on the Navy front, and I dread another bombing assault on the ships.

Tuesday 1st June, 1982

Happy Lunaversary! [*the First of any month, being the monthly anniversary of our wedding.*] We are safely home again, and fighting our consciences – the garden and sun call, but we must prepare for friends to lunch tomorrow. Bim has done all the shearing of the new grass, and we must put up the netting today. Three flowers the size of dinner plates on the clematis in the tub! The others all coming on well.

Off to walk Toad, so I'll bung this in the post. Love from us all, especially Marc! J xxx

[*Squiggles from Marc*]

1st June
    On the gunline in Volunteer Bay. Destroyed radar station on Salvador Hill. CW Alarm faulty. 0730 return to screen as EW picket. 1230-1500 RAS(L) with RFA TIDESPRING into very rough seas, including a change of course of 180 degrees. "highly dangerous" is CO's description in his report to Commander in Chief. 1800 detach to gunline in Volunteer Bay. (Wind W F5, SS4. 352 miles)

CHAPTER 9

REPLENISHMENT AT SEA (RAS)

I RECOGNISED AT the time – and it has remained true over these last 25 years – that the greatest scars I would bear from the war would not be from the fighting but rather the replenishing.

Over those three or so months of operations all our food, stores, ammunition and fuel had to come from ships, most of them from the Royal Fleet Auxiliary (RFA), equipped with their specialist derricks, winches and flight decks. Some, however, were merchant ships that had been hastily converted at the start of the war. While normal cruising conditions would give an endurance of fuel for some five days, and food for up to a month, the pace of our operations and the requirement to keep topped up with as much as possible to give us maximum flexibility meant that we would replenish every 24 hours or so in at least one of the three areas: RAS (S) for Stores; RAS (A) for Ammunition; and RAS (L) for Liquids.

I have described earlier our nail-biting RAS(L) on the way south, and then our collision while zig-zagging at Action Stations. These were perhaps just tasters for what was in store ahead of us! In the early days of the operation, while escorting the CBG and its clutch of RFAs and Merchantmen, we would leave the screen under cover of darkness to take up waiting station a quarter of a mile astern of the replenishing ship. This

In the waiting station at dusk. The tanker has its hose rigged outboard and is signalling by light that she is ready for the approach.

would all be done as the force zig-zagged with ships fully darkened and a minimum use of radar. We were attempting to be invisible to potential enemy submarines. Our communications with the replenishing ship were normally by a red signal lamp. When the ship was ready it could flash to us and we would then increase our speed to 22 knots, 10 knots above the replenishment speed, to drive the frigate up alongside the much bigger ship, leaving a gap of about 100 feet between the two. Once alongside, the Captain – who "had the con" (that is, he was personally giving the conning orders to the helmsman) – would adjust both the speed and the course to maintain the correct position, and when the two ships were steady, a gunline would be fired from a rifle to send a light nylon line between the two ships. This was attached to a heavier line, pulled across by hand, and in turn this heavier line would then be connected to a

Signal Lamp on bridge wing.

The gunner's party having fired the gunline across.

capstan to pull across the heavy jackstay. If replenishing fuel, the large and heavy hose would be heaved across the gap and – with effort – connected up to a fuelling position onboard *Ambuscade*. Once all this had been successfully completed, we would order, by flashing a signal by light, the tanker to start pumping. If uninterrupted, it might take some three quarters of an hour to pump the fuel. Once topped-up (the tanks onboard being 'dipped' or measured by the specialised stokers responsible), we would reverse the process and return, bit by bit, all the equipment to the mother ship.

For a RAS(A) or (S) there was a different routine and we would erect a large stump-mast on the flight deck (an evolution in itself!), which would act as a high point from which to attach a jackstay. In this case, the initial procedure was similar to that of a RAS(L) except that the heavy wire jackstay, once connected to the top of the mast, would then serve as the means of running a block or traveller between the two ships, pulled backwards and forwards by inhaul and outhaul ropes. With some six men on one of these outhauls, the mechanical winch would take most of the weight, but it required dextrous work on deck. Once this was connected and proved safe, the stores would be slung in a net or on pallets below the traveller, to be hauled across and dropped down onto the flight deck at the foot of the mast. That is when the work started for another team, who had to get in, unhook the

Replenishing liquids from a tanker in calm seas.

load and clear it away off the flight deck. It was then moved manually through the ship to be put in the store rooms, the large fridges or, in the case of ammunition, into the magazines. I have memories of some of these replenishments lasting for over six hours.

So much for a description of the mechanics of these evolutions. I have simplified the description of what inevitably are complex operations in themselves, but ones for which our navy had trained for decades and had (as we have today) very considerable skills. Now I need to give a taste of the reality of operating in the South Atlantic and in a war zone, with all the normal peacetime elements removed.

Above all else, our operations were dominated by the weather. When the winds blew they could come from the Antarctic unimpeded, whipping up the seas into huge waves that would have been deemed unsuitable for replenishment in peacetime. While the winds, rain and spray made for numbing exposure for those on the upper deck, especially the exposed forecastle, it was the rough seas that made for the excitement and danger.

Maintaining a steady course was impossible, certainly for a small, lively frigate trying to keep in station alongside the much larger ship which itself was not particularly steady on course, and which was either rolling from side to side or pitching from bow to stern. In peacetime one could pick an optimum course to steer for a replenishment to give the most stable platform, but in a war the operations dictated where the force was heading, and the constant zig-zagging then imposed further complications. No sooner had we become accustomed to the behaviour of the ships on one course than we would have to change again. Two ships alongside each other on a steady course were far too easy a target for any enemy submarine – in darkness or light.

If the seas were from the beam, the ships would roll – not in unison but normally in opposition. So the rig attached between them would at one moment be bar-taut, and the next go slack. The loads slung between it, or the loops of hoses, would therefore be in danger of being dragged through the water or alternatively flung high in the air. The RFA would seek to keep the tension correct as best as possible, but the conditions, particularly in the receiving, smaller ship, were frequently hazardous. At night time we operated just with low, red lighting to see what we were doing, and this increased the difficulty yet further.

For the Captain, conning from the bridge wing with the navigating officer alongside him, these replenishments demanded the highest skills in ship handling. His conning orders to the helmsman inside would be passed every few seconds to alter either the course (Steer 232... Steer 231......Steer 230" and so on to keep parallel to the mother ship) or the speed ("Set lever 46......Set lever 48" to vary the engine power of the gas turbines, which in its turn changed the number of revolutions each minute that the propeller blades turned). Close alongside, there could be no room for dropping concentration for even a few seconds. If the waves were from ahead or astern the ships would dip their bows in, and in particularly rough seas the propellers might even be momentarily exposed above the waves as the stern rose. If the waves were from astern, the lighter frigate could surf on a large wave and surge ahead. So either way, the speeds would not be constant and the course not always accurate. Whatever happened, we would be the one required to alter course and speed to maintain our position as best we could. It was a continuous and often exhausting process which continued throughout the entire replenishment until the refueling gear was returned to the tanker and the frigate sped back to its patrolling duties

But there were other factors to exacerbate the tricky situation. Each ship, as it travels through the water, creates zones of pressure and suction, the former at the bow and stern, the latter midships. These zones act rather like magnets. If balanced pressure zone to pressure zone, they will repel; pressure zone to suction zone, however, will attract. The danger to two ships alongside each other has long been recognised, and manoeuvres perfected to overcome them. Normally ships would operate with bows abeam each other, though with frigates at around two thirds the length of the RFAs and with tonnages of perhaps less than 10% of the larger ship, it was not always easy to hold the ship in position against these pressure forces. However, we went one stage further to complicate matters in *Ambuscade*.

Our normal RAS(L) position was to the forecastle by the 4½ inch gun, but we found this position unsuitable for two reasons: the gun could not be fired throughout the evolution, and the replenishment team of some 25 were so exposed to the elements (something we experienced in spadefuls in our initial RASs) that we considered it potentially dangerous to continue in this manner unless operationally vital. Therefore we took the decision to RAS(L) to the secondary position, that on the flight deck. That inevitably meant that the ship had to station herself another one hundred and fifty-odd feet further forward, resulting in our position on the tanker being unbalanced by us often being midships to the tanker's bow. The pressure-suction effect had to be fought as well as the elements.

So for the countless hours alongside, which add up to days – indeed weeks – the play between the ship handling and manoeuvring elements and its effects on the replenishment rigs often proved nerve-wracking. There were times that we came very close to the tanker, striving to find a parallel course, and then slowly, cautiously edging out again, while the derricks from the tanker stood in danger of hitting our masts, the hoses dragging in the sea and the solid loads disappearing from sight. Apart from that first day, we never touched again, but there were anxious moments. And then there were times that we either surged ahead or dropped astern, or pulled apart far too far, when I was concerned that the rigs would part. If this happened, under huge forces, there would be very considerable damage to equipment, and potential danger to the crews standing alongside at their stations. So worried was I on a number of occasions that I would clear the flight deck of all personnel and await the inevitable (which wasn't inevitable, because it never came about!).

So those were the elements we were fighting, but there was an enemy too, and there were frequent interruptions to our RASing when the ship went to Action Stations to be ready for an attack. Either sonar contacts, radar contacts or Electronic Warfare detections might trigger off such preparations. If this was the case, an emergency breakaway would be initiated by a series of short blasts on the ship's sirens. Immediately we would stop pumping fuel, or bringing across stores, and prepare in short time to release all the equipment in an abbreviated procedure that often left some gear onboard us rather than returning it to the mother ship. The jackstay would be slipped, and the frigate would proceed at speed to resume her screening station to protect the main body of ships from the incoming threat. For us dismantling all the equipment there were alarming moments as the seas crashed across the decks.   Not surprisingly, when exposed we wore lifelines to keep us onboard. But sometimes the alarms were false, and then we would start the whole procedure all over again...

It was not always rough, and indeed there were times of light winds and fog. Thick fog. So thick that during one RAS with the liner *Canberra* and RFA *Olna*, we completed an entire replenishment alongside her without actually seeing her! Quite a feat at 100 yards off, but we positioned ourselves purely on the angle of the lines that were attached to both ships. Incidentally, for our Captain to know exactly how far apart the ships are in a RAS, there is a Distance Line between the ships, held by hand by two sailors on the forecastle, right in the eyes of the ship, to keep it taut. The distances are marked by different-coloured flags at 20-metre distances. Red, Yellow, Blue, White, Green (RYBWG – remembered from Dartmouth as Rub Your Balls With Grease, so I can still remember the order of colours!). At night time, the flags were supplemented by little lights that could just be seen from the bridge. A crude but effective way of keeping the distance, and one where you can quickly see whether you are opening or closing on the mother ship.

Waiting to replenish from RFA *Olna*, with
Canberra on her port side connected to a refueling hose.
A marker buoy is streamed astern of the tanker.

2nd June

0400-0630 Naval Gunfire Support (NGS)
Volunteer Bay. NGS not called for (we
wonder if Shore Spotter is safe). 0630
return to screen. Helicopter tail rotor
gearbox unserviceable. Warning issued that
Argentine Exocet shore battery has been
established. 1725-1732 Action Stations. 4
helo transfers during day. Olympus main
engines giving trouble; concern about fuel
quality and availability of fuel filters in
Fleet, 1800 detach for gunline (Wind N
F5/6, SS4. 479 miles)

LIFE AT SEA IN WAR

"What was it actually like to fight a war?" We would be asked this often in the immediate months after our return. One would shrug, give a couple of light anecdotes and move on. Our experiences seemed rather irrelevant to the world, and these things were better kept to ourselves. It may well be best to keep up this policy now, and indeed many of the details will have sunk deeper than my recall allows, but let me pull out a few memories.

I have described how we prepared the ship for war in Gibraltar, stripping it down to bare necessities. Throughout the time thereafter we kept the ship secured for action. That meant that no loose bit whatsoever could be left out in any space, be it an office, cabin, mess deck or machinery space. Every single item had to be stowed away or tied down by rope. The theory behind this is to stop these items becoming either a missile if the ship was hit, or a subsequent hindrance to pumps if the ship was flooded and needed pumping out. Now the Navy had frequently practised "Securing for Action" with exercises and damage control drills, but none of us had experienced this tough regime for week after week, month after month. Self-discipline was vital, but frequent checks or 'rounds' were the routine to ensure the highest standards were maintained. I was the officer on board responsible for this, along with all routine matters of running the ship efficiently on a day-by-day basis.

We were all dressed identically, with key personnel having yellow surcoats with their role in large letters across the back. XO was mine, but I also attached striped epaulettes to my shoulders to denote my position. The theory was that in action, if the ship was in darkness or filled with smoke, my position in a key role of authority needed to stand out to all around.

We wore white overalls that had been impregnated with a chemical to make them non-flammable. The danger of personnel being in a fire or explosion with bare skin exposed has long been known to be a hazard in ships, and so the Royal Navy had for many decades used anti-flash hoods and gloves as protection. We constantly wore an anti-flash hood around our neck, and on going to Action Stations this was pulled over our heads, leaving only our eyes exposed. We carried long anti-flash gloves, again to be donned at action stations. Our trousers were tucked into our woollen socks (nylon burns, so nylon clothing was banned). Around our waists we wore an inflatable lifejacket on a belt (this lifejacket was the size of a small 6 x 4 x 4 -inch packet, and managed to make sure it snagged on all our surroundings). On the same belt was attached a survival suit – to be donned if we abandoned ship – again the size of the lifejacket. Field dressing bandages were also taped to the belt, and the officers then had additional packages which contained morphine, to be injected into any badly-injured personnel if we suffered casualties. Finally, we carried our Anti Gas Respirator (AGR), either on its own sling or also attached to the belt. This was 12 x 9 x 5 inches. Initially we felt pretty awkward with all this paraphernalia, but by the end of the war it was just an extension of our body. We took off the belt with its accoutrements, and the AGR and our boots, to go to bed, but remained otherwise fully dressed.

We slept in regulation sleeping bags that were tied to our mattresses, which in turn were tied to the bunks. So rough were the seas that I remember sliding from side to side within my shiny sleeping bag, hitting the bunk boards that prevented me from being tossed out. There were times that I lashed myself into the bunk to try and stop this uncomfortable motion. The one luxury I owned on board was a little tape recorder wedged into the corner above the bunk. I had half a dozen tapes rapidly gathered together before I left the UK, and these I would play in an attempt to lull myself to sleep. The usual one I went out to was Beethoven's Rasamovsky Quartets: pieces of music that even today bring back haunting memories of both our situation in the South Atlantic, and, even more, my yearning and love for my family back home.

Of course, there was very little time in one's bunk, or 'pit' as it was known. While the Captain was tied almost entirely to the Bridge or the Operations Room, the First Lieutenant had to go out and about all around the ship. My aim was to visit every compartment of the ship each day. Not only was I checking for the security and cleanliness of the ship but also, and far more importantly, I was seeking to meet every member of the ship's company face to face. It was very important to me to check out how everyone was faring in this unusual situation, and to keep my finger on the pulse of the rumours or buzzes that inevitably swept around the ship.

With half of the ship's company up and working at any one time, personnel would be scattered throughout the ship. Some forty or so were in Damage Control Parties sited both forward and aft, with their equipment at immediate notice to combat fires or floods should we be hit. Throughout the operation *Ambuscade* was kept in a much higher state of preparation, and this included the ship itself. She was divided into watertight compartments between the decks and between the bulkheads, or walls. This honeycomb structure was designed to prevent the spread of fire, smoke or flood. In peacetime (State Xray) the doors and hatches in the main thoroughfare are left open to allow easy access. However, there are two levels of increased security. The next level up (State Yankee) was the one we were operating at in our wartime defence watches. Doors between bulkheads were closed and kept watertight by eight clips around the perimeter. There was, however, a relaxation to allow only two clips to be fastened on frequently-used doors in this state. Hatches between decks were dropped into place and had eight screw nuts holding them down, but in the centre of each was a kidney hatch, a smaller hatch some 18 x 24 inches that was again capable of being clipped watertight. These kidney hatches, barely big enough for a man to struggle through (especially in combat gear), were again left open. Come Action Stations and the highest degree of readiness (State Zulu), all doors and hatches had to be fully closed and clipped. Yet, whichever state we were in, my job was very much one of roving through the ship despite these impediments, and literally dozens of doors and hatches. So another memory of the war for me was the constant battle with clips – first taking them off to go through and then clipping them on again. The kidney hatches were the greatest struggle, for one would climb a ladder to the hatch above, knock off the clips, heave open the heavy hatch and then launch oneself through, normally getting one's lifejacket or AGR stuck in it as one wriggled through.

An added complication for me was my cracked rib. It was painful, but there was nothing to be done and only time was going to right it. I dared not take any painkiller for fear of being affected by the sedative, but both opening those clips and lying wedged into my bunk in the rough weather were far from comfortable.

Although one takes it all for granted, the sheer motion in a ship operating in rough seas has one braced all the time, hanging on to something to steady oneself, with muscles tensed. No, it was not relaxing, but I suppose it kept me fit, for I suspect I walked miles, climbed mountains (or their equivalent), and certainly exercised my arm muscles.

HMS Ambuscade.   2/6

Dear Louisa and Marc,
I thought you would like a picture of me, fully dressed. Don't I look funny? I sleep in these clothes, but don't have the hood over my head very often.

Thank you for your Fathers' Day card. Very nicely drawn.

Look after your marvellous Mummy. Lots of love, Daddy

Darlingest J, At long last some mail – lovely to hear from you 16, 17, 18 May. What a long time ago it seems – you had just got the buzz that we were on the way down here, and yet it seems as though we have been here for ever.

The BEEB says Stanley is surrounded, as indeed it is, but what happens next we haven't a clue. Will they surrender (I doubt it) or fight to the end? Will we shove them out or have a frontal assault? Will there be a big naval battle soon?

We were again in action last night and twice went to action

stations today – for spurious reasons as it turned out. It all certainly gets the adrenalin going... As did the replenishment yesterday – in very rough conditions, daylight thank goodness, but particularly hairy. Puts years on me in one afternoon, but I'm not going grey yet. We set off yet again for tonight's mission; all go.

Lovely to hear all your news my darling. The garden sounds as tho' it's flourishing; I hope you're not doing too much. I never did finish the fruit cage, but I hope it's not too difficult. I love hearing all about it. Glad the weather has been good. Hope I don't miss it all. Who knows. Why don't you have a week in Wales with Bim during school hols (perhaps at the end, just in case I'm back) and plan to keep another week for us when I'm back. You never know, we might be back Aug / Sep – there's not a clue, but we can't stay here for ever – can we??

Keep looking after yourself, and don't work too hard. Send everyone my regards etc. etc. I'm not writing any other letters!! Happy B'day to Peter tomorrow!

Keep smiling, be brave, and I'll be back before you know it. We might find it's all over in a week.

Give a big kiss to L and M, stroke A and J, and imagine a lot more for yourself!

I love you beyond description. J

Westbourne, West Sussex.   *2nd June, 1982*

Hellow, Hellow, Hellow! Let's hope this letter reaches you <u>soon</u>. Otherwise I shall feel moved to write to Maggie Thatcher to complain that she is not looking after your moral welfare. And how is your physical welfare going – lost much weight on your restricted diet??

We have had a lovely hot day, with kids splashing in pool and all adults feeling really rather hot. Iain had the day off to go to the Derby, but he chose to come to us instead – very flattering. He was v. interesting on the activities of the paratroops and their colonel in the Falklands – it's nice to have a military outlook and things explained.

Lunch was rather late, because guess what! Prince Charles rang up at one o'clock! He had tried before, it seems, but I had been away. He says you wrote a long letter from Ascension and he has written back – so I said Wot abaht _my_ letter? (telling him all about who was in what ship) and he said he hasn't got it yet. So I filled him in on what I could and he told me BG was XO of _Antelope_, which I hadn't realised – and he also told me how worried he was about his brother, and how he doesn't get letters from him either! He asked for J's address and I gave it, and then we agreed to go to visit him in his new quarters in Kensington Palace for tea on June 23! I shall just take Wee, and leave Bee and Jerbs with I and L, which will be nice.

Here is a space to tell you how much I adore you. And miss you.

I am trying to license the car but can't find the Registration Document – any ideas? Not in any of our files. Wee's school fees also need paying: £155, but the extras make it £200.50. Ballet £6 also due. Can we cope??

MJ has just rung to check on me – sends love. He thinks ships will just return and turn round to go out again – rather disappointing. Will you get _any_ summer?

I think Alfonso has just done his first jerk. How thrilling! I expect he wants to send his love, as I do. Every bit of it. Jx

3rd June

    0250 on gunline, no call for fire.
    Visibility 200 yards. Return to screen as
    EW picket, cancelled RAS(A). Commenced
    scrubbing fuel tanks to help solve problem
    with filters. Steaming on one engine to
    reduce fuel flow. Took charge of MV IRIS
    who was joining the force, by guiding her
    into her station in the middle of the

```
fleet (no radar, no lights, in dark and in
fog). (Wind light and variable, SS2. 341
miles)
```

Westbourne, West Sussex.   *3rd June, 1982*

My darling one, Another day goes past. News that some are returning from Down There, and me wondering how long it will be before the imprisonment ends for you. MJ in any case thinks it will be a question of coming back, having about 6 weeks here, and returning south. That sounds terribly disappointing! You'd better get sunk – but make sure everyone has their lifejacket handy.

The South Atlantic fund to help dependents of casualties is now over £1,000,000.

4th June

Suddenly overtaken by heat and humidity last night – fell asleep! It is amazingly hot – I doubt if you can have any concept of it in your wintry conditions! First broad beans ready, and peas waiting to plump out ready for eating. First lettuces starting to bolt, second lot nearly ready to eat. How I wish you were here!

The Canadians arrive to stay with your Ma today. We may go to the theatre tomorrow, which would be nice. I have booked seats for a couple of Festival things on 8th and 14th July – of course, if you are home I know somebody will give up their seat for you!

The full car service cost only £69, including £7 for 'repairs to exhaust' – is there no end to this? Anyway, the usual cost is £100 for a full service and MOT and all the bits, so I am quite happy. I have had to pay our £83 gas bill – I am told it is far less than most people's, which averaged out at £100 – £120 – they have taken to overprinting the bills with "Please remember the exceptionally hard winter", as so many people have complained. But our last bill (estimated) was £44, and the chap said it was a ridiculous estimate. Ah well, what's money?? Got the buggy done

– new wheels at the back and new cross-strut for £12.45 – not bad, I thought.

Our neighbour has just been in to invite me for supper on Tuesday, and to offer J's services – Stacks of men are offering their services, but I can't accept!! Do come home soon, my darling – I'm sure you need mollycoddling, and I want to smother you with love. I miss you so terribly. J xxx

4th June
    Overnight patrolling in vicinity of RFA
    OLNA awaiting RAS(L). 1135 close up for
    RAS, MV CANBERRA replenishes first 1500
    first line passed 1700 RAS complete, all
    in thick fog with visibility of less than
    half mile, sometimes down to 50 yards.
    1900 Action Stations. 1920 Helo ops.
    Overnight screening CBG. (Winds NE F3,
    SS3-4. 323 miles)

HMS Ambuscade.   4/6

Darling one, There's rumour of more mail being in the fleet for us, but fog yesterday stopped it being transferred and now no-one claims to have it…. No doubt they will find it and I will have another letter from my beloved wife. It is lovely hearing from you, and that you are safe and well. I love hearing all the minute detail of your life, the children, garden et al.

We have had a relatively quiet couple of days, standing by for this and that, rigging for the other, but not actually carrying out very much. At the moment am dressed in 2 jerseys and foul weather gear waiting to do a RAS liquids – refuel – it's 10.30 but still pitch dark. Dawn comes at about 1100 and dusk at about 2100. A strange day but it does mean that I can get on with the more mundane things before light, when we are far more likely to be attacked. It's a bit like the lull before the storm, I expect that there will be much more action before it's all over, but who knows – they <u>might</u> give up and withdraw. Even after that I can see that ships will have to remain down here for long periods, together with a big garrison on the island. It seems the whole navy is involved, or will be. What is it costing the country – 100s of billions?

Talking of billions, I received my pay accounts today. £426 end of May, and will be £565 at end of June. Latter includes back pay, separation allowance and £1 day South Atlantic. Monthly pay thereafter should hover around £460 – after allotments. So I think we are in calmer economic waters!

Are we??! Darlingest, go and buy yourself nice things, and the children. Cheer yourselves up with a lovely splurge and see how much you can spend. Christie's painting? Garden chair? Fruit cage? Climbing frame? I'm sure if I was there I'd find something, but must rely on you to find the next gadget or two! I mean it.

Don't know when this will fly off – will be able to send a 31-word free shipgram today (and every 14 days) which will probably overtake it. Love to everyone, but all my love to you. J

MODMAIL FAMILYGRAM SERVICE

FIRST FREE FORTNIGHTLY FRATERNAL FREIGHT FROM FERVENT FRIEND FELICITOUS FEELINGS FROM FAR FLUNG FIRMAMENTS FUTURE FETE FROLICKING FROWSTY FRUCTIFICATION FEASIBLE FANCY FLIGHT FORCOM FORMATION FAREWELL FOR FORTNIGHT FROM FELICITOUS JOHN

Westbourne, West Sussex.   *4th June, 1982*

My dearest husband, I've had a long talk with B tonight, (he's off duty and at home) and he tells me you are well and safe, but that you will have some amazing tales to tell! He was absolutely popping to tell me all about it, but didn't dare over the phone – but at least it sounds as if you are on occasion having an exciting time! Goody goody – I'd much rather you were doing something interesting and not just sitting next to *Hermes* or *Invincible* and pinging for submarines. He also told me the Type 21s were breaking up, but unfortunately you won't be coming back for repair. I gather there is no hope of seeing you for at least a couple of months , but I hardly expected to. He also told me that mail was being dropped much more often, which greatly pleases me, and that censorship is not in force as far as he knows. So please can we have some nice purple passages and some scurrilous gossip about the ship?? I hear the weather is <u>foul</u> – poor you. Here it is so hot and humid that all our sticky things, like towel holders and sticky pads, are dropping off the wall every two minutes. But the broad beans like it, and I have had several strawberries.

I had a lovely time planting out my last few tomatoes, spinach beet, alyssum and marigolds this afternoon, as Marc took himself off to bed (refusing all lunch or anything to eat all day) and slept for 1 1/2 hours! So I also had a nice rest in the sun, you'll be glad to hear.

I got my free copy of *Navy News* today, with never a hint of *Ambuscade* in it, but it did tell us that HMS *Torquay* is the oldest serving ship in the Fleet, and that she is commanded by FM. Did you know?

We had tea with Caroline and the kids today – a great pleasure for all, apart from the lodger labrador Guinness, who kept jumping on top of Marc. All the children played very well together, which was super.

PS Do you know where the Gannex-backed rug is??

Time for bed. How I wish you were here to cool it down for me! Take great care, my darling. I love you. J x

157

HMS Ambuscade. 4/6

Dear Louisa and Marc, This is what my ship looks like

I've told Mummy to buy you a present each (Lego?) Would you both buy her one, please? Ask her to lend you some of my money!

Look after everyone. Looking forward to seeing you soon. Lots of love from Daddy

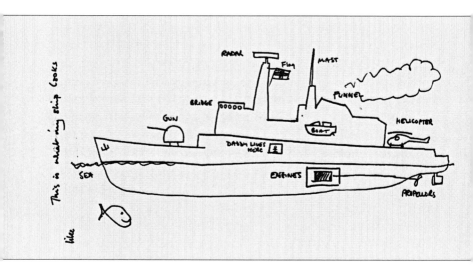

5th June
1136 sunrise.1150 helo check test flight,
1200-2100 helo ops. 1932 Sunset. Overnight
screening. (Wind N light, SS3, visibility
500 yards. 365 miles)

HMS Ambuscade. Sat 5/6

Beloved J, Another letter, as there will be a collection around the Fleet at midday by a helicopter and then a ship will be departing later in the day.

In an attempt to bring back some normality last night we showed a film in the WR – a comedy – the first film shown since the night *Sheffield* was lost. Inevitably, 3 minutes into it we went to Action Stations! However, we managed to get back to it and it was a good break. The Squadron Padre arrived in the middle of it, so that interrupted it yet again. He's here for a week.

How can I describe life onboard? The ship basically works in 2 watches; half the ship's company on watch at any one time, and able to fight the ship until the rest arrive. Watches are 0800 – 1300 – 1800 – 0100 – 0800, so pretty tiring, but everyone is coping. The times of changeover mean a late lunch and a very early supper – 1730!! Funny how the stomach gets used to it, and actually expects it at that time. I find myself getting up at 0645 and going to bed about midnight – that's on a day when there is no special requirement for anything from me. Other times I have been staying up for most of the night and going to sleep for a couple of hours before lunch. So it's all flexible but manageable. Food remaining good. Shredded wheat / fruit juice / poached egg, bacon and sausage / ½ slice bread and Oxford marmalade is my standard b'fast. Lunch is a snack – usually 1 slice of toast with cheese and baked beans, and supper which is soup / starter, 1 choice main, and pud. Cheese board is surprisingly good, tho' not up to our standards! So we do pretty well.

Will run out of nutty [*sailors' slang for sweets*] in the canteen in a week, but that doesn't affect me (apart form the odd tube of polos and extra strong).

We live in our action gear, so I normally wear overalls, tucked into my one pair of black wool socks (or 2 borrowed massive white thick socks) with pusser's string vest and white jersey. We sleep in this and tumble in and out of our pits as required. We have everything except a parachute strung around our waists – just in case.

Does this give just a little glimpse into our strange existence? I love you totally. J

HELICOPTER OPERATIONS

From the very start, our helicopter proved an essential element of our armoury. Flown by the Pilot, fought by the Observer, and with an occasional additional crew member as a winchman for particular missions, our Lynx helicopter was modern and exceptionally capable and versatile. It could scout ahead with its radar and electronic warfare sensors, it could act as a communications relay platform, it could carry out covert visual searches and it could carry out attack operations. Against submarines it could drop torpedoes, having been guided above the submarine's position by the helicopter controller onboard using our own sonar contact, or by controllers in other ships or in the Sea King helicopters that hovered ahead of the force with their own dipping sonars in the water beneath them. In shallow water, depth charges could be used instead.

Helicopter Pilot's view of Frigate during approach.

Recovering our Lynx Helicopter.

However, the brand new weapon that was introduced at the start of the Falklands war was the Sea Skua air-to-surface missile for attacking ships. I have memories of these missiles, hastily brought into service ahead of the normal peacetime procurement programme, being dropped to us by parachute from RAF aircraft, presumably based on Ascension Island. The missile was instantly put into operation during the early fighting and used to good effect against small Argentine craft operating in inshore waters. Four separate attacks by other units were achieved during the operation, but we never had the occasion to use ours.

The versatility of the helicopter itself was enormous. It was used for spotting during Naval Gunfire Support when we were bombarding shore positions and, as already described, it became increasingly involved in night-time operations ashore, inserting and extracting Special Forces as the advance across the

Island progressed. Our Pilot loved this element, having been a "Jungly" (a Royal Marine Commando specialist). The helicopter was also used for transferring urgent stores or personnel from ship to ship when necessary. Additionally we had Chaff on board it to lay as a decoy if the force came under missile attack, and this was used on more than one occasion.

Back onboard, the helicopter was supported by its own team of maintainers to keep this complex machine fully operational. The mechanics and electronics of the machine and its sensors kept the team very busy. After failures, much hard work – often in severe weather conditions – had to be carried out to get the helicopter serviceable again. Unusually, on the way south, two main engines had had to be replaced onboard and these evolutions were followed by Check Test Flights so that the Senior Maintenance Rating could certify the helicopter safe to fly. For a number of reasons, the Flight had a succession of three aircraft to work on during Operation Corporate, and that itself caused a considerable extra workload.

Maintainer working on Helicopter's engine, while stowed in the hanger. He is wearing full anti-flash and all the survival gear—including his plastic mug!

High seas threaten to sweep across the flight deck.

As well as carrying out the maintenance, the Flight personnel doubled as the Flight Deck crew, under the supervision of the Flight Deck Officer (FDO – either the Supply Officer or the Master at Arms), who batted the helicopter on or off the deck at launch and recovery. The wind direction and speed had to be within specific limits, and the deck motion, the rolling and pitching, also had to be within tolerance. So it became a matter of fine judgement for the Officer of the Watch on the bridge to select and maintain the optimum course for the minimum time to launch or recover, and for the FDO to choose the best time to lift off or land. Once lashed on deck, the missiles or torpedoes could be moved out on trolleys to be hoisted up onto the launchers under the helicopter. It was precision work for all, working as a team in often appalling weather conditions, and very frequently in total darkness, save for a couple of hand-held torches with red filters.

Helicopter lift-off under Flight Deck Officer's control.

The one Helicopter Controller onboard, a Leading Seaman (Radar), had immense responsibility for the control and safety of the helicopter. (Off watch, he doubled as the ship's able cartoonist, illustrating our internal paper "Pistol Post"). Based in the Operations Room on his dedicated radar with his specific radio, the Helicopter Controller's duties were of a magnitude such that ten years before they would have been carried out by a Lieutenant. While a member of the Ship's Flight, he was a fully integrated and utterly essential member of the Warfare team. With such individual responsibilities, the Helicopter Controller was one of the most sleep-deprived people onboard.

6th June
> 0215 launch helo. 1200-1630 Helo ops
> Detach from screen for gunline with HMS
> ACTIVE in radio silence. (Wind N F2
> increasing gale 8 SS3/5. 385 miles)

HMS Ambuscade.   6/6

My darling, Mail closed 5 minutes ago but they're holding it for me. A helo leaves in a min, so all I've time to say is that I love you and that is the most important thing in the world to me.

You are the focus of my life and I couldn't be happier than having it that way. This strange situation we are in just emphasises the point and makes it all the clearer. It's a shame you are in such a dreadful position, not knowing what is happening to me. What I do know is that this mail arrives so long after that any action I'm about to go into will have long been reported to you.

Meanwhile we all hold together and I'm happy with the feeling onboard and I think it's going well. One day we'll get back, and to a normal life. When, who knows, but I long for it, and to be with you and the family again.

I love you J

7th June
> 0400 NGS in Bluff Cove, close inshore
> with HMS ACTIVE. Fired 85 rounds. Hit
> ammunition dump. Ship's stabilisers
> unserviceable (and remained so thereafter)
> Return to CBG. 0731-0755 Action Stations.
> 1140 sunrise. 1220-1500 helo ops. 1700-
> 1810 RAS(L) RFA OLNA, in bad weather and
> into heavy seas with no stabilisers.
> Captain describes RAS to Commander in

Chief as "very hairy". Main engines
proving increasingly unreliable. 1830-2000
helo ops.
Overnight escort MV ATLANTIC CAUSEWAY,
RFAs ENGADINE and OLNA, plus minesweepers
(converted fishing vessels) CORDELLA, PICT
and JUNELLA into San Carlos TA. (AOA now
renamed Transport Area (TA)). (Wind NW,
F5, SS4. 405 miles)

AMMUNITIONING SHIP

As we fell into the nightly scene of shore bombardment, so came the routine of returning to the CBG to replenish, with ammunition being the top priority so that we could return for the next night's operation. While it normally came by jackstay alongside, (as described on page 141) there were times when helicopter transfers were used, with underslung loads of 4.5 shells. The benefit of being able to respond more rapidly to a threat was obvious. Having been up all night steaming inshore for a bombardment, the speed and efficacy of carrying out the replenishments was always a top priority. The Captain might then achieve a little sleep, leaving the ship in my temporary command.

One RAS(A) I recall had us ammunitioning from both a jackstay on the forecastle – with Chaff missiles coming onboard – and on the Flight Deck, where 4½ inch shells were being unloaded. These would all then be carried by individuals through the ship to the appropriate magazines or 'ready-use lockers'. The force came under the threat of attack yet again, the inevitable 'Emergency Breakaway' sounded and we closed up as usual at our Action Stations. I had literally hundreds of shells and missiles scattered through the ship, and in our rush to secure we thrust them into cabins and offices, lashing them down, to return to after any action. There was no subsequent action, but

Wessex Helicopter with underslung load transferring ammunition.

we were kept at the High Alert state for some while. Now, post had arrived from the UK via that stores ship, and had been transferred across by jackstay. The eager Postie took advantage of the lull in the action to start sorting the mail out, and the official mail was delivered up to the Bridge where both the Captain and I were. Well do I remember an official letter from a senior officer in our base port, Plymouth. He had signed it off to us very many weeks beforehand, and in it was an official rebuke on the results we had had (well before I arrived, I understand) from an Explosive Safety Inspection. The ship had been found to have two clips missing on one of our Ready Use lockers for the Chaff missiles. Outrageous! Suitably rebuked, I had to smile at this great peacetime breach of safety regulations, when here we were, at Action Stations, under threat of air attack, with live ammunition scattered through the ship.

The place, unable to keep in the right position. Me with some 20 men looking after the hose inboard on the flight deck. Have to heave it across some 200 feet of tempestuous seas + connect up + then worry about getting rid of it all in a hurry if the ship gets out of control or we come under attack. It's amazing no one has been hurt yet. Doing it in the dark makes it even more jumpy!

HMS Ambuscade. 7/6

My darlingest J, Time flies by, which is no bad thing for me. Yesterday was remarkably quiet with no activity internal or external. I even got on with some report writing! Had a Communion service with some 30 – 40 ship's company, which is a pretty good turnout.

Overnight we were busy on a mission which was pretty noisy gun-wise, and then we went to Action Stations at breakfast time when it appeared that we were under attack. That fizzled out and the main activity of the day was a RAS(L) – replenishment at sea liquids! – which took all afternoon, and as usual was somewhat hairy. We were bouncing all over the place, unable to keep in the right position. Me with some 20 men looking after the hose inboard on the flight deck. Have to heave it across some 200 feet of tempestuous seas and connect up and then worry about getting rid of it all in a hurry if the ship gets out of control or we come under attack. It's amazing no-one has been hurt yet. Doing it in the dark makes it even more jumpy!

How are you my darling? Is Alfonso developing fast and are you happy in your pregnancy? You mustn't allow Alf to be miserable, so keep smiling and singing. What books are you reading? I look forward to seeing the new photos you've promised, and I enjoy having the old ones around my cabin. Does cheer me up no end.

Thinking of how you could spend all this money we are getting – is the porch a possibility?

Hope to get mail pretty soon and may be quite a lot of it. Do hope so – keep writing, I love it and it does all bring you that much closer. What a long way 8,000 miles is. I love you. Take care. J

Westbourne, West Sussex.   *Monday, 7th June*

My darling one, Gosh how I missed you yesterday! After running the creche for church, we came back to go for a walk and Louisa collapsed with heat stroke. Then S and C arrived for a surprise visit, and as soon as they had gone, the Canadians and your mother arrived for lunch. So I was spooning aspirin down Louisa, washing lettuces, pouring drinks and getting lunch together all at once, and I wanted you so badly! However, all was well in the end, and we had a very pleasant afternoon in the sun with Wee sleeping inside most of the time. She is better today, but still running a temperature and off school. Marc is fighting fit, and he adores the beaver he was brought – it's a large fluffy toy with a pocket up the front so it can also be used as a hand puppet. Wee also had a nice present. I was helped to net the currants, rasps and strawberries – all v, necessary, as they are starting to ripen.

Sorry about this pen – the children have used it and wrecked it, and I can't use another as I am in hospital waiting for antenatal attendance. I skipped the queue because I misheard

'Jennifer Phillimore' for me – but it's still a jolly long wait on my back. I weigh 9 stone now, and elephantiasis of the bottom and bosom has set in. But I still don't look particularly pregnant, I'm glad to say.

Later : All is well at hospital – no suggestion of spina bifida, and I have decided against amniocentesis for Down's syndrome – after all, if the test did prove positive I would be in such a tizzy with you so far away, so we'll leave it.

Children insisting on writing to you , so here they are!

LOUISA   xxxx   MARC xxxx   and all my love from ME Jxxxxxx

8th June

0445 R/V HMS PENELOPE together with MVs ELK and NORLAND to escort back to CBG. Minesweepers too slow and cannot complete passage in darkness, so escort them back too. 0510 Helo ops 1147 sunrise. 1200-1430 helo ops. 1630-1910 Vertrep ammunition from RFA FORT GRANGE, stationed on her beam at 500 yards, but "very tricky" (describes the CO) given state of our engines and our minimum speed of 12 knots. 1706-2045 Action Stations in anticipation of air attack on CBG. 2030 sunset. (Wind NW, F5, SS4. 317 miles)

Inshore, RFAs SIR GALAHAD (with the Welsh Guards still onboard) and SIR TRISTRAM, and HMS PLYMOUTH are hit by bombs. Heavy casualties from this action, with 50 killed or missing and 57 wounded, mainly from bad burns.

Westbourne, West Sussex.   *Tuesday, 8th June, 1982*

My darling, This letter should be in Red, as it is obviously a red-letter day when I write to you from Bognor Regis! We are at Zootopia with the Playgroup for their summer outing – not a bad little park with loads of animals, including a tiger, a seal, and a single lonely penguin. Also a railway, and battery-operated boats on a reasonable-sized lake. It started off sizzling hot, but thankfully the weather has cooled down a bit – we were wilting after 20 minutes! I still have Wee at home – she was not well yesterday, so I kept her home, but she perked up so much in the afternoon that I decided all was well. However, high temperature again this morning, and all she wants is pints of water.

Back home again now – this letter is looking decidedly scruffy, but I hope it reminds you of home.

I go out to supper tonight, and it is lovely to be able to take our first big ripe strawberries instead of an expensive box of chocolates. J has been invited too, though she is preparing for A's return on Saturday on the *QE2*. I have had to crush a bitter pang of jealousy, but I know that you would hate to have to return that way, especially before the job was finished, so I must be grateful that you are at least having an interesting and exciting time!

Pause to move the hose round the garden. The hose is getting old and is splitting in several places. We may have to indulge ourselves <u>again.</u>

(Short lyrical passage on the beauty of the philadelphus, now in full white blossom.)

Wednesday a.m.

Darlingest one – letters and a family gram today all combine to put me in highest good humour!! Oh how I love you, and the sooner you can hold to your vow to love and cherish me, the better. I <u>hate</u> to think of you coming under attack, but trust that God and good training will bring you safely through. The children hope you will shave before returning! They would love another picture from you. Darling one, take care. J xxx

On screen close to Flagship, HMS *Hermes* as a
Sea Harrier approaches to land on.

9th June

Overnight on screen. Helo ops. Detach to
TRALA. R/V MV STENA SEASPREAD. Helo and
boat transfers. Carry out machinery
repairs with assistance from Fleet
Maintenance Group. 1100 revert to Damage
Control State Xray (doors and hatches open
— fresh air invades ship for first time
since Ascension Island.) Operate deep fat
fryer; CHIPS !! Change Defence Watch
routine: previously 7/5/5/7 hour long
watches, now 6/6/6/6 hour, for remainder
of operation, (Wind NW F4/5, SS3 184
miles)

CHAPTER 10

MAIN ENGINE
PROBLEMS

W E HAD BEEN dogged with problems with our main engines throughout the operation. Both the Olympus (the civilian version of which powered Concord) and the Tyne engines, marinised version of the jet engines used in aircraft, were proving sensitive to the quality of fuel, which was found to be variable. The conditions of the South Atlantic meant that the rough weather was stirring up the tanks more than usual. We were also replenishing from a wide variety of tankers and it seemed to us that the purity of fuel was questionable at times. While more modern ships had a method of making the fuel more pure before use, the Type 21s depended only on fuel filters, and these became first scarce, and then near impossible to find replacements for. We resorted, yet again, to the terribly demanding manual scrubbing out of the fuel tanks in order to clean out the impurities, but this was not working. By 8th June the Captain described the ship's situation as follows:

- Port Tyne unserviceable (u/s) since 15 May
- Port variable pitch propeller pump on emergency only; electric pump u/s
- Starboard Tyne exhaust fan u/s
- Starboard Olympus fuel control u/s
- Stabilisers u/s

The combined result of these defects was that we only had one effective engine, and were obliged to keep above a minimum speed of 12 knots to maintain all the required mechanical services. More in-depth repairs were called for. Our Squadron Marine Engineer Officer arrived on 9th June, and we detached to an area well to the east of the Falklands, named the 'Tug, Repair and Logistic Area (TRALA)', which was deemed to be safe from immediate attack. There we had assistance from a Fleet Maintenance Group on board MV *Sena Seaspread*. We progressed the tank cleaning and most the repairs were completed in around 12 hours.

10th June
    0720 Repairs complete (except Port Tyne
    main engine and stabilisers remain
    unserviceable) and fast passage to return
    to CBG. Damage Control State Zulu (all
    doors/hatches closed). 1134 sunrise. Helo
    ops. 1300-1750 RAS(L) RFA OLMEDA. 1820
    Helo ops R/V RFA BLUE ROVER and escort to
    TA. (Wind N F5, SS3/4. 295 miles)

HMS Ambuscade.   *10/6*

My darlingest J, Another day passes – hard to catch up with which day it is for they all go past as one. We have our ups and downs, and have gone through a difficult period with one of our senior officers – not the Captain! – being ill. Very touchy subject, so no more and no speculation at all, but it adds to the overall pressure.

We are not allowed to write about our activities, our whereabouts, or state, so, as ever, it makes it difficult to describe what we are doing!! We expect to take on stores and ammunition overnight tonight – that involves the whole ship's company for some 4 or 5 hours, and we will be taking on fuel as well. All calls for a lot of seamanship and hard work. Organising is hard because plans change in seconds and rarely are fulfilled according to instructions. I now usually wait until the very last minute before commencing any preparations. We have got ready so many times for something only to have it cancelled or postponed!

Hopefully, by the time you receive this letter the war will be largely over, but who knows what the future holds. Will they go on fighting even if they have no troops on the ground in the FI? Will the Junta fall? You probably know better than I can guess from our limited sources of info. Are you watching the box a lot?

Must dash this off to the mail box. Things progress.

I love you more than you will ever know. J

11th June
    0330 R/v HMS PENELOPE, escort RFAs FORT GRANGE and OLNA and MV BALTIC FERRY to CBG.1218 R/v with RAF Hercules for airdrop, then return to screen. RAS (Stores) cancelled (Wind NW F5, SS3. 447miles)

HMS Ambuscade.   11/6

My darling one J, Another day goes by. Now 0830; this is the quietest time of the day – doesn't get light until 1100 or so and little activity going on. The Captain sleeps until about 1300 most days, and I take the ship. Because of our many activities during the night he has quite a few disturbances which I don't.

We get a new senior officer today. One went off to the Flagship yesterday for medical examination and isn't to return. He is the one I referred to yesterday. Has taken the whole war badly and got increasingly depressed and pessimistic. Our Force's senior officers began to realise we had a problem – but it wasn't a ship's material one! So, it's a blow and happened

Looking dead ahead from the bridge during a gale,
with *Ambuscade* rolling to 20 degrees.
There were times that 45 degrees of roll were recorded!

suddenly, although looking back one can piece a few bits of the
jigsaw together. Overall I'm not too worried, for I found him a
drag on my attempts to keep things buoyant – and on the morale
of the Wardroom. So hopefully it may get better; but it inevitably
has an upsetting influence. No doubt he will be flown back to the
UK, so you had better only admit to knowing that he left "on
medical grounds" if you are chatting to other wives.

Never fear – I'm <u>not</u> going the same way and feel very sane
and safe, if not very sanguine. There is not too much humour in
our business at the moment, and it is difficult to be light-hearted.
We are a fairly serious lot, doing a somewhat serious thing.
People are also very tired and are showing it.

So much for us (we are holding together and doing well, despite all) – how about all of you? I long for our next mail – whenever that is – and to hear all about your life. It does help bring us together over these 8,000 miles.

Do give all the right messages to those I ought to be writing to. I will one day, but need inspiration, which is far away at the moment.

Much better that I devote all my spare time to you. I love you always. J

Westbourne, West Sussex.   *Friday 11th June, 1982*

My darling one, The QE2 has just got back, and I am feeling thoroughly selfish, self-pitying, suicidal and depressed beyond belief. J says she would far rather face the thought of a year alone than have A lose his ship – but I'm sure she doesn't realise that this is what we probably <u>are</u> facing. I heard last night that when you do get back (and no guesses when, though Sept. / Oct. sounds likely), you'll only have time to cut your hair and mend your socks before you go out again. It means that we shall be together for only 6 weeks in the year – and, oh darling, I want you so much. I'm sure I should be writing cheerful little notes to keep your morale up, but I hardly ever get like this, and after all you are my best friend and the only person I can really talk to about this. At the moment I hate the Argentines even more than I hate slugs, and that is saying everything. Marc asked me last night whether I was crying "because Daddy doesn't love you any more?" Louisa's voice from top bunk: "Of course he does. In this family we all love each other." They are being so sweet and comforting – but I do wish you could see them growing up, and I wish they could see enough of you to know you as more than a name.

And now I shall stop being dramatic and tell you how they are growing up, in that Marc went to play-school today by himself for the first time. His face was a picture when I went to collect him – a smile from ear to ear, and intense pride in his little offerings, and he slipped off to play when I left him, quite happily. So did Jerbs, who has evidently missed her morning stroll – and she is still somewhere on the common!

Louisa didn't really recover until yesterday (Thursday), but she managed school on Wed. morning and a birthday party in the afternoon for a girl called from school, with two brothers with outlandish names. It was up near Petersfield, so I took a group, and while James and Wee went to their party, we went off to the Queen Elizabeth country park for a marvellous walk and a picnic tea. Then a dash back and frantic organisation to get children ready for bed and me for the theatre to see Valmouth. It was a musical, very slight, but well done, and we had a delicious supper afterwards at the Charcoal Grill. Several of the cast also came in, which was fun. I got back at midnight, which followed another late night out at supper the evening before. That was all very nice, except that we were given salt to put on our strawberries!

Which leads me to the garden. I froze broad beans and rhubarb yesterday, and this morning I finished weeding the flower garden and put weed preventer all over it. Let's hope it works! The tin can idea has preserved our tomato plants, which were otherwise disappearing overnight, and they are now strong and healthy. And even the dahlias, of which I had despaired, are now sprouting. The currants and some raspberries are turning colour, and some runner beans are half-way up their poles or wires. I decided to use garden wire instead of string on the beanmaster.

It rained last night for the first time for weeks and weeks , which saved me some work. (Catastrophe – Marc has just discovered his "Sticking" from school in the wastepaper basket! It was just a piece of pink paper with glue on it – no pictures or anything – but he is v. upset! He has decided that he would like to send you his picture.)

B when he rang told me more about what you are up to, so that I can picture you. He also told me what I had worked out from your letter about the missile attack, and he filled me in on the details – to be kept strictly to myself. What an experience! He said the First Officer of the other ship will have a word or two for PM! I also heard that the ship is not coping too well with the weather, which could faintly possibly bring you back earlier, though he also said you would probably get repaired down there. How I wish the politicians could sort something out and announce that a UN naval force would take over!

I feel much better after writing to you – and the last letters (21, 24, 25 May and Familygram) were very cheering. Have you abandoned censorship yet? If not, B says to his knowledge you are the only ship applying it! But you sound freer in what you write, so perhaps you have at least been spared that duty. It is sweet of you to be so understanding on the worrying aspect – though at present it sounds as though the families of the troops are the ones who have to do most of the worrying. They have still not released details of the *Sir Tristram* and *Sir Galahad*, and it all sounds very grim.

Alfonso seems well, and on Wednesday I am sure he was telling me that he was enjoying Valmouth. He didn't make me feel at all faint, which reassures me for the two Concerts and the play about Edith Cavell that I have booked for when the parents come. Westbourne mums have started to recognise my maternity gear, but it's still such a little bump that no-one has been at all sure until they asked today!

B says he could find out when you will return if he delved, but it is so highly classified that he doesn't really want to know. But at least I feel that someone somewhere is planning that you shall come back (unlike Jerbs, who is evidently <u>not</u> planning to come back till supper time!), and we shall have a jamboree! Some of the returners on the *QE2* (shown live on TV) were to my mind quite tepid about it all, and I shall be boiling with enthusiasm. Darling one, take care. I miss you so frightfully, and love you so unalterably passionately. Jx

MORALE

A short few words on a huge subject; one that is key to success in any military venture. While I can only comment upon the morale in one small unit among the hundreds both afloat and ashore, I suspect it will echo the experiences of many others.

Overall, as my letters generally reflect, morale onboard was high. That is a sweeping statement that is not 100% accurate, in that there were individuals, at varying seniorities, who were gloomy and indeed pessimistic about the situation and our chances of survival. Left unchecked, those people could have undue influence, so they needed to be contained in subtle ways. But overall the mood was good, and the determination to succeed was dominant. Belief in our ability to fight and win, confidence in our Captain and the warfare team to do the right thing, were present throughout. Reliance on the professionalism of the entire crew was absolute, and it was indeed a well-honed team.

Beyond our own fighting ability, probably the next most important factor influencing morale, certainly at the start, was the justification for going to fight. Here we were, going to war with an enemy we took to be fairly friendly until a few months before. Without being too moralistic, I believe we did run through the thoughts of what constitutes a Just War, and we concluded that this operation met the criteria. A foreign country had invaded a British Territory, albeit one that not many had heard of or really cared for. The inhabitants, holders of British passports, objected and wanted us to rescue them. What was paramount was that it appeared that the British public fully supported our actions. Knowing this mood back home, reflected in various ways by all the press, was a huge boost. (In our various forays since 1982 into foreign wars, especially the second war in Iraq, I have a feeling of sympathy for the troops going to fight for the country, knowing the extent of public opposition to the action, and the questioning of the legality of the war).

The ship's company of *Ambuscade* was a team: we called

ourselves the Ambusmen. The engineers kept us going against many odds and without the planned maintenance programmes in force. The Weapons Engineers kept our armament and sensors fully operational, rather than having their regular maintenance days where they could fine-tune their equipment for many hours; these were demanding times which called for improvisation and new routines. It was not easy for the engineers, both mechanical and weapon-and-electrical, to adjust to this, for they could spend days with their specialist equipment operating at maximum efficiency and not requiring their support. Then they were suddenly thrust under huge pressure when the equipment failed.

Ambuscade made a trip to the logistic area (TRALA) for repairs, as I have just recounted, and this brief spell enabled a few hours of greater relaxation. The Damage Control state could be dropped to allow doors and hatches to be opened and fresh air to pervade the ship. But, more importantly, we could have chips!

If an army marches on its stomach, a navy (or certainly the Royal Navy in those days) sailed on its chips. But in the Damage Control condition in which we had been operating since leaving Ascension Island, the deep fat fryer had been drained and turned off. We could not afford to have boiling fat onboard if we stood to be attacked; the danger of it being sprayed around after an explosion was too great.

Food was an essential ingredient of morale. The chefs worked in two watches to produce food all around the 24-hour day: the meal in the middle of the night as watches changed was just as important as that in the middle of the day. Snacks at other times helped supplement the major meals. Variety, interest, colour and taste were as essential as the freshness and nutritional value. The time for communal eating, at whatever hour, to snatch a few minutes of time in the company of others was a vital ingredient of the social life onboard. The chefs did magnificently throughout, but the chips in the TRALA produced hours of 100% morale!

The Supply department carried out a wide variety of tasks beyond the cooking and catering. The stores accountants looked after tens of thousands of items that were needed through the 24-hour day to keep us running. The small team of stewards was the backbone of the First Aid parties under the direction of the Medical Officer and his professional assistant. Another part of our morale-boosting set-up was the shop we had onboard, manned by the NAAFI. (This is the Naval, Army and Air Force Institution, manned by civilians, although for the duration of the conflict they were required to wear uniform and come under the Naval Discipline Act.) Although tiny in size, it stocked an incredible variety of essential ingredients from cigarettes, writing paper and washing powder to... Nutty, as chocolate and sweets were called. Having a few luxuries in life became increasingly important in our time away from home, and the joy of a bar of chocolate was out of proportion to most other things. While there was not much onboard, we could normally buy one Mars Bar or Dairy Milk each day. News reached us from other ships that their NAAFI had run out of nutty; perhaps we were the only ship down south still to sell it! Our cunning NAAFI manager, who with his young assistant ran the shop, was a remarkable, aged man who had survived torpedoes and sinking (three times, if we were to believe him) in the Second World War. Without telling us, he had been quietly rationing the nutty from the time we left Gibraltar. Taking pity on another ship that was in company with us at some stage, I sent across a bar to the Jimmy, who was a particular friend of mine. We had served together 10 or more years before, and shared the same birthday. The birthday was coming up shortly, so it seemed appropriate – and slightly one-up!

We were lucky to have our Squadron Padre onboard for almost the entire duration, and he played a vital part in the maintenance of morale. He, like me, would rove the ship constantly, but he, unlike me, could sit for hours in the various mess decks as their friend, chatting over the situation, listening to their worries, talking about their families. While I expected to talk to every individual during my rounds of the ship, my conversations were necessarily brief because of the situation. But I could normally tell by an individual's tone, or by eye contact, if something was wrong. If I had a concern I could ask the Padre to look out for that person, or have a word with the Divisional Officer to take a closer interest. It was again teamwork in the careful oversight of people as individuals. That said, both the Padre and the Doctor kept all their confidences to themselves in a most professional manner.

The role of religion onboard at this time was interesting but not surprising. I remember a remarkable turnout for a Sunday service on the Flight Deck (we were still in the tropics heading south) after *Sheffield* was sunk. The Captain led the service, I read a lesson and there was considerable emotion and reflective thought – particularly for our loved ones at home rather than for ourselves. Later, after the Padre had joined, we had regular services which were very well attended, in the Junior Ratings' Dining Hall. The 'Organ, Portable, Small' (an electric keyboard) was played to accompany the hymns and we sang with gusto. Whatever our own individual faith, these services were vital ingredients to our overall morale.

12th June
　　0700-0900 RAS(L) with RFA TIDESPRING. 1136 Sunrise. 1315 Vertrep stores. 1555-1703 Action Stations for expected missile attack. 1950 Close up for RAS(S) with RFA RESOURCE, 2350 pass gear and commence replenishment by Jackstay. (Wind SW, F4, SS3. 391 miles)

HMS Ambuscade.   *12/6*

My darlingest J, Well, we are still here; just fallen out from action stations, the expected attack failed to reach us. Now dashing off, in company with 3 others to spend a night close to where it all will be happening. By the time you get this it will be old news, but I can't describe our operations until it's all over – by which time I no doubt will have no intention of talking about it anyway! I'll listen to the news in a minute and that may tell me how much I can pass on.

Took fuel this morning in the dark, fairly calm for a change. We were going to do a big RAS (S) but that changed, because of the threat, and has been postponed indefinitely – until peace? So we've run out of bacon and nutty (not that I eat the latter!).

News is that Argentina says that we are attacking Port Stanley and that MOD is saying nothing... look back to my first paragraph! Let us hope that they surrender soon to prevent the bloodbath that it could so easily be. More naval casualties from this morning, but could have been far worse.

Have a new senior officer on loan, with another bound south i.d.c. Not entirely satisfactory, but can do nothing. Present chap seems good news, so it would be a shame to change again. He was a Head of Department in this ship 2 years ago, and the guy coming down was the last one – so it's kept in the family!

Won't it be lovely to finish this business and get home to you. We all long for that so much. Of course the danger is that we come back, sort ourselves out over a few weeks and set off south again – not a thought worth dwelling on, but quite on the cards (– not for general promulgation / discussion between wives, please!...). I suspect PM is extremely disciplined in what he writes home, and that self-censoring is rigid. Therefore, beware knowing!

How I shall enjoy being back with you, to look after you and love loving you. I'm totally optimistic about getting back, but less so on timing of return. I wonder how long these letters are taking to reach you? There has been no real exchange of correspondence yet because it really is taking over 6 weeks to get a letter out and back – I guess. What a bore, but might possibly get better when we have Stanley airfield.

I am yours for ever and beyond, and love you more than you will ever know. J

13th June

0427 Break away from RAS after 5 hours alongside, 56 loads transferred. Whole ship's company evolution to strike stores below decks throughout night. Return to screen. 1142 sunrise. 1330 close range weapons firing exercise. 1515-1620 helo ops. 1820-1911 Action Stations for possible air raid. Detach from screen to R/V with HMS ACTIVE then 25 knot passage to gunline for NGS.
(Wind SW F3 SS3. 348 miles)

Westbourne, West Sussex.   *Sunday, 13th June, 1982*

Hello, my darling! Surprise, surprise – JB rang a little while ago to suggest that I sent a letter via her husband, so let's hope it gets to you nice and quickly, and on a day when you don't get deluged by a thousand others just arriving.

We have had a jolly day today – Marc cracked the back of his head open by falling against the angle of the wall by the breakfast table. It didn't bleed too much, so we went via the Family Service and delivered tissues and toothpaste for Poland (apparently that's what they need!) and then went on to casualty. Marc took fright at the sight of the south Indian doctor, and screamed blue murder in the X-ray room where they insisted on sending him – I had to keep out of the way because of Alfonso. However, they let me cuddle him while he had 3 stitches put in (they could have used steri-strip, but it would have necessitated shaving his head), and he was angelically good. He seems totally unaffected, and when we went to see your mother, he was leaping off the table on the patio with all his usual glee. Your ma gave us lunch, as we didn't get out of casualty till 1 o'clock – she seemed delighted by the intrusion.

Nathaniel's christening is on 4th July, so your ma and Rhoda are going down. Tom is not well again, and they fear that this time it may be the dreaded rheumatic fever – it all sounds rather grim, but surely God must look with favour on such a godly couple?? I said to Maggie on the phone that I felt awfully sorry for God – each time we hear a ship has been hit, he must be inundated with instantaneous, "Please God, let it not be <u>my</u> husband's!", and I got a little talk on the fact that He has suffered so much for us that He understands perfectly.

I am planning a Treat for Self tomorrow – Wee is going out to tea with a little friend, so I am tucking Bee into his buggy and after dropping the school crowd off at Compton we are jumping on the train at Petersfield (£2.60 return with railcard!) and going to the India exhibitions at the V&A and the Hayward Gallery. It won't be ideal with Bee, but he will be company, and I don't want to thrust him on Julia and I doubt if he would be happy elsewhere. I anticipate that he will sleep through at least one exhibition – he went to bed at 9.30 tonight, after falling soundly asleep in the car today!

Alfonso is making little pressing touches – not really kicks, but experimental stretches, it seems. He is still wonderfully wee – if I keep this up, I won't have too much weight to shed afterwards and will return to my sylph-like proportions in about two days!!

We need you to mend the cupboard door of the white china cupboard – Marc swang on it, and broke the hinge-holders off. I have mended it quite successfully, but I am sure you can do better. And you'd better come home soon anyway, as the children had the first two pea-pods today; we are picking a bowl of strawberries daily, and the first courgettes are the size of my

Louisa and Marc waiting at home

thumb! Darling one, it will be so magical (your homecoming, not the courgette!), and I long for it. It does make a delightful daydream, and I am grateful for having such a nice imaginary yet real day to fantasise about. I adore you and long to prove it. J xxx

14th June

0125-0700 Action Stations. Ship in Ultra Quiet State. 0325-0545 NGS in Berkley Sound. Inside minefield and Exocet danger area, in company with HMS GLAMORGAN, YARMOUTH and AVENGER. AMBUSCADE fires 228 rounds in support of 2 Para on Wireless Ridge, Sapper Hill and Stanley airfield. Two 155mm batteries destroyed. 2 Para make substantial advance to outskirts of Port Stanley. 0700 return to CBG. 1300-1630 helo ops, vertrep ammunition. 1645-1745 RAS(L) RFA TIDESPRING. 1845 Wasp helo

**lands on deck, ship rolled, Flight
Observer fell out of helicopter into
safety nets on side of flight deck.
Narrowly saved from going overboard.
Screening station. 2000 26 knot passage to
gunline to join with HMS PLYMOUTH,
YARMOUTH and AVENGER. (Wind SE, Force 9
increasing SS6. Miles 437)**

CRACKING UP

The high seas and the fast speeds that were required for operations started taking a toll on the ships down south. Day after day we pounded into the seas, either patrolling our sectors in a defensive screen around the large and important ships, or darting in and out to the Islands themselves to carry out another operation. All ships suffered to varying degrees, but the Type 21 frigates such as ours literally started cracking up.

We were not the first to notice it, but news got about fast that hairline cracks amidships were appearing at the level of the upper deck. We had a steel hull up to that deck, and then an aluminium superstructure above it as a fairly continuous block from the bridge down to the Flight hangar. Recognising that all ships bend and flex at sea, the ship architects had designed a flexible joint into that upper structure, called 'the hockey stick' because of its appearance. But the hull itself was expected to remain fully intact. The strains of the South Atlantic operations over the many weeks were too much.

The structural integrity of the main hull was paramount to the safety of the ship and, although the hairline cracks (one either side) that appeared were miniscule and did not leak water, the import of their appearance was enormous. What were the chances of the ship literally breaking in two? No-one knew, but the Royal Corps of Naval Constructors back in the UK put their thinking caps on. We were not too impressed by their signals

Ploughing into the sea.

back down south. We were to monitor daily the length of the cracks and report back home.

Not wishing to make anything of this onboard, we kept the records and watched as the cracks extended downwards, very slowly but surely, each day. Although not unduly worried, there were times when I became particularly anxious about the effects of speed and weather. Our dashes at dusk into coastal water for Shore Bombardment, and back out again at dawn, were perhaps the most worrying, and we would not have dreamed of putting on such high speed in peacetime. Imagine yourself standing between decks near the bow of the ship. You are going up in an elevator, say three floors, but pause for a second and then crash down direct to ground level, shuddering to a halt. The ship slows momentarily, shaking and reverberating noisily through its entire length, before the bow again lifts to the next wave. The pounding is incessant; how long can a ship – all three and a half thousand tons of it – take such a hammering? I would wander down several times a night after a particularly violent judder to see the effects. Frequently I would find the ship's Shipwright – the 'Chippy' – there first, with his torch and ruler.

Eventually the Naval Constructors in the UK told us that we needed strengthening longitudinally, and that iron beams the size of railway sleepers were to be bolted onto the upper deck amidships – but only when operations permitted.

Later, when the Argentines had surrendered and the threat had been removed, we went alongside the repair ship *Stena Seaspread* at anchor in San Carlos water. Our engineers were a bit worried about this solution, for it meant drilling lots of holes to bolt the beam into position, and these holes might weaken the hull more than the cracks. After a lengthy and heated debate with the engineers 'down South' and those in the UK, it was decided that our cracks would be welded up, and that the beams would be attached only after our arrival back home. Highly specialist naval engineers from the Fleet Maintenance Group carried out this welding task

Obviously we survived, but it certainly was another worry at the time. It was part of the realities of wartime operations for what had been a peacetime, albeit hardworking, exercising and ocean-going navy.

HMS Ambuscade.   *14/6*

My darlingest girl, Another quick letter before I turn in – now 2300 – got 2 hours sleep last night and a very busy day. Spent last night at action stations blatting hell out of Stanley. A massacre, I imagine, as our troops closed in. Then back during the forenoon – RAS Ammunition for 3 hrs this afternoon in freezing conditions, followed immediately by refuelling. Now doing 28 knots back in a force 10 and rolling all <u>over</u> the place. Terrible motion and not much chance of sleeping, however tired. Back on the gunline this evening, but hope not to have to fire. The news (BEEB) seems to be that they have surrendered – or ceased fire, at least. We therefore will be there tonight "just in case". Let us hope and pray that by the time this reaches you the battle is over – in the FI anyway. But will it go on from the mainland and at sea? What will the wretched Argies do now? Time will tell, but quickly, I hope.

Haven't had any mail for ages and ages. Do hope all is well with all. I'm terrible at not writing to parents but just can't get into starting at this stage. Perhaps when it's all over, but where do you start describing all this? Meanwhile, send them all my love, reassure them that I'm fine and apologise that I haven't written yet. Give them any news you can drag out of my ramblings!

Much nicer just chatting to you in this way and hoping that it brings me just a little closer to you. I ought to be writing to the children too, but not this time. Give them my love, and tell them how much you mean to me. Let's pray for peace.

I love you for ever.J

Westbourne, West Sussex.   *14th June, 1982*

My darling one – Hoorah for this ceasefire! They've just announced it, and although I don't trust our dear opponents an inch, at least it means you are less likely to have tons of trash dropped on you by a passing transport plane.

Darling, I have had a super day in London! It started badly – "Good morning, this is Radio 3 on Monday, 14th June". "Good God," cried I, sitting bolt upright in bed, "The Hayward Gallery exhibition closed yesterday!" However, I only missed sculptures and pictures, and instead I went to the Museum of Mankind in Piccadilly, where they have re-created an Indian village in Gujarat – It was quite amazingly authentic, and quite stunningly well done, and although it was only small, I was very impressed. There was also an exhibition on Asante on the African Gold Coast – we would call it Ashanti – which was quite fascinating.

And all free! I shall definitely patronise the Museum of Mankind again – quite wonderfully high standards.

(Pause to goggle at the box to see pictures of the landings at San Carlos and so on – up till now we have only had a map to gaze at. They are also showing the troops arriving back in Argentina: they could easily be interchanged with the pictures of the British ditto, and no-one would know or feel the difference – clinging wives, weeping mums, clapping dads – it's all the same.) Back to London, and Mughal Art and Heritage at the V&A. It was lovely and I enjoyed it so much. Marc was awfully good – he sat in his buggy and ate a lollipop and some raisins for some of the time, and enjoyed things like the huge gold tiger's head from Tipu Sultan's throne. Otherwise I used him as an object to make comments to when I felt particularly excited about some of the exquisite things on display, and he responded by telling me that there were lights down under the grating on the floor. I did so wish you had been there, as I think no-one could have failed to be excited by it all, and I should have enjoyed reeling off my inadequate knowledge to you!

Then there was another (free) exhibition upstairs of pictures of India, and then we got a bus to Piccadilly. Marc fell asleep, so I went round the Museum of Mankind with him blotto , then back to catch the 3.18 train. Home to feed Jerbs, then a walk in Stoughton woods before collecting Wee from East Marden. A huge house with tennis court and horses and long private drive – not quite like ours! Wee returns on Friday for a birthday party, which is nice.

15th June

Some pressed flowers to make a Victory Bouquet for you, my darling! It all sounds so exciting – P and M even rang me up at 11.30 pm, so I am starting to believe in it all. How much brighter the future looks! I do adore you. Have fun. I love you. J xxx

15th June

Overnight it becomes obvious that
AMBUSCADE is unable to make gunline in
time for operation. Decide to return to
CBG and reverse course in Sea State 7.
Ship rolls to 45 degrees! CO writes in
his night order book "The weather is no.1
enemy. We are not yet at peace, therefore
keep your teams alert (no lookouts outside
until the weather improves). Do not alter
course without calling me first, keep
minimum speed or such that you keep
station and keep steerage way". Make slow
speed into gale. Take up screening sector
for remainder of day. (Wind S, Force 8-10,
SS7. 258 miles)

CHAPTER 11

SURRENDER

OUR FORCES were on the outskirts of Port Stanley, and we had been engaged in the nightly bombardments. Topped up again with ammunition after a RAS(A), we steamed back inshore again at high speed for further Naval Gunfire Support. The pounding and the shuddering had me worried yet again, and I prayed for an end to the fighting, if just to save the ship from breaking in half. Surely this had to be the last night of operations?

News gradually filtered through, I suspect from the radio frequencies we had established with the troops ashore whom we were heading to support, that white flags were starting to appear in Port Stanley itself. We kept going, hoping that we might have our mission cancelled to stop another punishing passage inshore. Eventually the rough weather beat us and we slowed down and then reversed course. It was hours later that the news was confirmed. The Argentine forces had surrendered. Mission complete: we had recaptured the Falkland Islands.

What had sometimes seemed a near-impossible task, at a distance of 8,000 miles and without routine support, had been achieved. However, there had been times when the outcome was not clear-cut – or not to us, anyway. We had the feeling, towards the end, that progress was too slow and that we were running out of ammunition to maintain the tempo of the assault. We had

Ambuscade's Battle Ensign flies proudly
alongside a flag hoist message.

lost ships and troops ashore, with grievous casualties – but now it was all over.

Strangely, I barely recall any reaction on board. Certainly there were no fireworks or champagne. We were relieved to have a lessening of the immediate tension, but we were suspicious that it could all flare up again and we were determined to keep our guard up to ensure that we were not to be caught out. We therefore kept our routines going; the Defence Watches, the loaded weapons, the Damage Control state of the ship, all continued as though nothing had happened. To keep everyone alert and motivated soon became our greatest challenge.

HMS Ambuscade.   *15/6*

Darlingest J, I'll start now, although little news from my last. By the time you get this you will know far more than I do now. It would appear that Stanley has surrendered and an amazing number of Argies was found there. Otherwise we have no news. We have been battling out a Force 10 in mountainous seas and snowstorms. Very dramatic and particularly uncomfortable. Our stabilisers bust some long time ago so we are rolling around madly. We concentrate on surviving this rather than anything too warlike.

16/6

Calmed down a bit and not too bad now. Had the chance to go out on deck and assess the damage. Guardrails and fittings totally carried away in places and quite a few cracks in the ship.

We wait to hear what the next step will be. Will we be required to go into disaster relief? We have signalled to say we have an experienced team onboard!! It would be good to <u>see</u> the Islands we have been fighting for… Has Arg. given up the war??? Time will tell, but it's going to be <u>very</u> boring sitting out here. Time flew when the action was on, but now…

Meanwhile I'm emptying my in-tray; some paperwork goes on and lot of report writing. My usual job of 'heads and bathrooms' – traditional peacetime role of XO – has not been attended to!

I actually found myself singing in the shower last night – and having the shower in daylight – unheard of before because of the likelihood of attack. So things must be looking up. Still sleep fully clothed and have masses of things around our waist.

My darling one, I love you so much and am longing to be back with you. When I don't know, but soon, please. Love to L and M, and all my love to you. J

16th June

Patrolling sector on screen of CBG in very rough seas. Some flying operations and mail transfers. All talk is of a ceasefire but nothing heard officially. Have to be fully alert to threat though there is a feeling it is all over. (Wind S, F7, SS7 decreasing 4. 199 miles)

From Captain's night order book "Stay alert — keep your teams exercised and not run down. Look outs are to be posted GDP etc when it is not raining/snowing. We are not at peace yet".

HMS Ambuscade.   *16/6*

Dear Louisa and Marc,

It has been very rough and <u>snowing!</u> Isn't that a funny thing to happen in the summer?

I hope that it is sunny and dry with you, and that you are able to play in your swimming pool. Are you helping Mummy with watering the garden (I hear it's the only reason she wants me back!)

How are you enjoying school, Louisa? Are you able to read a

little yet? Have you got lots of friends there? And Marc, are you enjoying Play School? Does Mummy help there very often?

We may get some letters this evening from our helicopter.

I hope that perhaps there will be some letters from you.

I miss you all very much indeed and look forward to seeing you as soon as I can.

Look after your marvellous Mummy. Lots of love, Daddy

Westbourne, West Sussex.   *Wednesday, 16th June*

My most darling one, I am stuffing myself with raspberries and strawberries with sugar and yoghurt – it is so utterly delicious that I do wish I could send you a mouthful!

I gave a lovely Victory Lunch today – various wives, children and grannies, and the strawberry pavlova with our strawbs was particularly outstanding. Everyone was in such a good mood now that it seems we may hope you are no longer in danger, so everything was as nice as could be.

B rang tonight – his last call, as he leaves Northwood for Bath now. He tells me you were pounding away during the (non) Battle of Port Stanley, but that you are still remarkably unscathed. Good news in a way, but it does put you at the bottom of the list to return! I suggested September as a possibility, and he said very likely. All I do hope Most Desperately is that you don't go off again afterwards! And that apparently depends on whether the Argentines promise to be good.

Thursday

Waited to see if the news was any more definite, but it seems that Galtieri is reluctant to sign away his political future. Ah well – many things could happen by September – but Alfonso won't be one of them! Heard the news of Baby F's arrival last night, so I will write today. My dearest one, I think of you constantly. All my love, J xxx

17th June
   Quiet day patrolling in screening sector
   around CBG. Flying ops throughout day.
   (Wind SW, F4,SS4. 298 miles)
   BBC World Service announces President
   Galteiri is deposed and that there are
   peace talks underway. CANBERRA embarks
   5ooo prisoners of war.

MAIL

Along with food, mail was the most emotive issue on the morale side. From Gibraltar onwards, its receipt was eagerly anticipated, but its delivery was spasmodic. Every means to get mail to us was sought out. Aircraft flights to Ascension Island, ships sailing south to join us, and even parachute drops all played their part. But then the mail would come in clumps and very frequently out of sequence. Sometimes there were distressingly few sacks, but at other times dozens of sacks might arrive, passed across during a RAS, perhaps, or underslung under a helicopter. They would be hastily carried below and, if operations permitted, then the letters would be sorted out into different piles for each of the messes. (These were the Wardroom, two Senior Rates' messes, and the half dozen or so Junior Rates' messes). The pipe on the main broadcast "Mail is now ready for collection from the Regulating Office" (the Leading Regulator being the Postie as well as the helmsman at Defence Watches) was normally greeted by cheers throughout the ship. It all took a frustrating length of time and even then, half the ship's company would be on watch and unable to read the letters until coming off watch; a tantalising number of hours of waiting to see if they had got any mail, while those off watch could rip open their letters to catch up with the latest from home.

I am sure we all had our individual routines, but mine was to get the letters into order by their postal date and then to speed-read through to check that there were no calamities reported. Then I would return to them at a quieter time to soak in the news and try to imagine life at home, seeing my wife and children through her words. It was always an intensely personal and meaningful time, with music playing quietly in my cabin. Strauss' "Four Last songs" or Beethoven's "Rasumosky Quartet" became ingrained in my mind and heart and remain so today. The musical connection to my family through my wife's wonderful letters was a hugely important factor. Reading our letters had the ship's company quietly absorbed in our own private worlds throughout the ship. But of course there were times when whole batches went missing, and we lost the continuity of news from home. So the narrative might launch us into an assumption that news from an earlier letter (an illness, a domestic disaster or whatever) had already been absorbed. That could have a very worrying effect on the individual. Further, the lack of any letter when all around you are reading theirs could be even more devastating. So while mail could be an overall morale booster, we had to be even more on the look-out for those who were adversely affected. From the Captain downwards, no-one was immune from these pressures and worries.

From the early days, free airmail letters became the standard form: a blue sheet some twelve inches long and five inches across, folded into thirds with four sections to write on, one for the address and one for the sender. Both Jenny and I had got into the routine of trying if possible to write one each day, and these letters were like gold dust, tucked away for re-reading in the days ahead until the next mail drop. Understandably we tried to remain cheerful and resolute, though this did not always succeed, as our correspondence may show.

Jenny would be keeping herself busy – and her friends made sure this was the case – even if bringing up two very small children and being pregnant with the third wasn't busy enough for a single parent. The garden was our passion, and her accounts of the summer plantings and harvesting helped me to envisage our terraced house with a river running alongside it in Westbourne, Sussex.

For myself, I did not want to worry Jenny or the children with the war, but I knew she would know far more of the details of the progress of the war than we did actually down there. Indeed, with the time delay in getting post home, with it waiting to be embarked in a ship sailing north and homewards, it seemed almost pointless to report anything about our progress. On top of that there was censorship of mail before it left the ship. I do not know if a general order went out across the Fleet to impose censorship, but *Ambuscade* imposed one in order to achieve operational security about our movements after leaving Gibraltar. Looking back at it, the censorship would appear rather meaningless, but we took it seriously at the time and I was required to read the mail of the officers and key senior ratings to ensure that no secrets or valuable information would get home. They in turn had to do the same for those under them. I have to admit now that I barely scanned the pages, for I was as keen to maintain their privacy as to maintain the country's secrets – and I never had to ask for anything to be deleted. We relaxed the rigid routine a while later but still insisted individuals refrained from reporting our whereabouts, forces in company and similar operational details. Because I had to set the standards and be purer than pure, I suspect that the self-censorship of my mail was the strictest onboard. Perhaps by publishing these letters that theory will be proved – or otherwise!

HMS Ambuscade.   *17/6*

My darlingest J, Mail from you last night – 3 letters, 20 /26 / 28, and card and letter 24 May. Super to hear from you after such a long time without any mail – and I hope some more may arrive tomorrow when another ship arrives down here. I see that the arrival of my letters on 28th made you miserable – I know the feeling – first contact just brings home the reality of the separation and war; they take getting used to.

Anyway, perhaps the news is rosier this evening. The President is ousted – although another hardliner has taken his place, but perhaps there can be a diplomatic solution. Who knows, but it is the only answer. We do need that guarantee of peace to be able to get on with the clearing up. At the moment we have to continue, expecting attacks but just slightly more relaxed – but only <u>very</u> slightly! (I actually had a pint of beer before dinner – unheard of!) but I have written to your parents, my ma, and Sarah, who very kindly wrote yesterday. Aren't I a good boy – I've been putting it off for so very long. Not that they are good letters, but it's the thought…

I love the photo of you 3 on the swings – it's a lovely one – thank you, I have all the photos above my desk / bunk, which is nice. Keep sending them! I never have enough.

I love also reading about all the little things of life – mud pies in the kitchen, the size of your peas, tummy, overdraft and so on. Do tell me all, however boring it seems to you.

Do I understand you have been with your parents? How are they and Bim? Are you off to Wales and when? I <u>do</u> hope we get a week there as a family when I get back – longing for it and will get leave (10 days minimum?) Future programme totally unknown – no clues at all. Will take some 3 weeks to return and will be kept v. hush until north of Ascension, so don't expect too much warning. Don't know if we will be turned around again after a short time in UK. Depends so much on how things develop. No promises – except that I expect a little leave! Don't breathe a word about this to <u>anyone,</u> the subject is not being mentioned or discussed. (I would hate you to know more than SM, as you might!)

Won't it be marvellous getting back to normality one day. Can't wait to see you, but will have to for now. I love you more than I can describe. Take care. J

Letter to Parents-in-law

HMS Ambuscade, Falklands   17/6

My dear Bun and Dick, Thank you so much for your letter and photographs. They arrived some 10 days ago, and were very much appreciated. I now have a little more time to write, for the immediate pressure of war seems to be off, although there is no confirmation of this. Writing is not made easy by the huge seas that are throwing the ship around like a cork. It's a Force 10 gale with some snow! I hope that your summer is somewhat better.

We have seen nearly 4 weeks of fighting; although we haven't been in 'bomb alley', we have been backwards and forwards to it escorting convoys, usually done under cover of darkness. Gunfire support of the troops ashore has been another night activity and we were there for the final assault. The rest of the time has been spent escorting the carriers, dodging missiles (too close, sometimes!) and replenishing fuel, stores and ammunition from alongside Fleet Auxiliaries – again often by night. So it's been pretty active.

The future seems very uncertain, and so we don't know our movements at all. It depends so much on the Argentinian reaction, so we stay glued to the BBC World Service, which crackles into life occasionally.

Do tell Francis Pym sometime how very impressed we have been with the political direction given to this. The Government has acted boldly and with excellent timing at every stage – without seeming too bellicose. Sounds pompous of me to say so, but I didn't think that politicians had it in them to be so resolute in war! Let us hope that the final solution is a political success, to follow up the interim military solution.

I hope that you are both well. I understand J and the children may be with you – or rather were about to be in my last letter. Much love, J

```
18th June
   On screen. 0800-0946 RAS(L) RFA
   TIDESPRING. 1150 sunrise. Flying ops
   through day. 1130-1240 Light jackstay
   transfer of stores from HMS ARROW before
   she returns to UK. (Wind SW. F3, SS2. 347
   miles)
```

HMS Ambuscade.   *18/6*

Darlingest one, A very quick note before I turn in. Yesterday morning they told us to RAS(S) (stores) and so we rigged the stump mast – a very heavy pole that sticks up on the flight deck. Something that is difficult to do and I always swore I wouldn't. No sooner was it ready than they said our RAS would be postponed till after peace! Fine, we unrigged and stowed. 2115 last night – RAS(S). So spent all night doing so, and got to bed at 0630! We now have enough food for another 2 months! What a business. Today, Communion service this morning (Padre leaves tomorrow) – a sleep – meetings, action stations for a raid that didn't come in, supper, bed now before most of the night at action stations when we go in off Stanley to bombard them again. I get the impression the advance is going well for us.

I wonder what sort of a Sunday you have had. Hard to think that it's summer with you and all is blooming (I hope – how is the garden?). I hope that you are making the most of it and spend lots of time just lying in the sun (?) reading hags' mags.

Longing for some mail, it seems such a long time since the last lot. Do want to hear all your news, but mainly that you are well and bearing up to the strain. I am.

Do you get these letters in a rush, I wonder, or in dribs and drabs… My life is so concentrated and narrow at the moment that there is little to relate. There is no time for relaxation, so I don't really need books, music or whatever. Music would be nice, but I don't think about it.

What a fabulous reunion it will be when we are together

again. Will we have a week in Wales? Are you off there, meanwhile, to see what it is like?

I love you and long for you. J

Westbourne, West Sussex.   *18th June, 1982*

My darling one, I feel it is high time that I had a nice little batch of these forms addressed to me! I long to hear how things are going for you, and how it feels to have a little peace and quiet in the skies. I still don't trust the Argentine military at all, but at least the abolition of Galtieri is a step towards peace. Most people round here, including your mother, seem to think you'll be on your way home now! No-one seems to have any grasp of the wider issues at all. It makes me wonder whether the support for the Conservatives, which is so strong now, will melt away as the Falklands slip from first place in the news. As it is, the World Cup is putting out the timing of the News, which annoys me intensely!

Nothing much has happened today, apart from some gardening while Marc was asleep after playschool. Every spot in the garden is now crammed full, and every conceivable space is planted with leeks! I seem to have grown a million of them – and I expect I shall pull a lot up thinking they are grass. I have now finished planting out everything, except for thinning out a row of french beans. It all seems terribly prolific, and I don't know how I am going to cope with it all! I picked another 2½ lbs. strawberries tonight, and I have decided to use them for jam instead of going out to buy jam strawbs... I shall do 3 small batches – I am sure we have enough, even though we all eat mounds of them.

Wee went to another birthday party this afternoon, with conjuror, Punch and Judy, giant balloons etc. – how do we compete? She came back so full of beans that it was 8 o'clock before we even went up to wash them! Tomorrow we have Marc's stitches out and see your ma. Must go to bed now. <u>Wish</u> you were here!! I do love you. Take great care of your precious self. J xxxxx

```
19th June
   On screen. Pm helo ops. (Wind SW, F5,
   SS4. 302 miles)
```

HMS Ambuscade.   *19/6*

My darlingest one, A letter before supper. The day gets off the
ground slowly – doesn't get light until 1100, but then we keep
going from early hours right through until late. Have actually
spent most of the day on paperwork. Brown pen working
overtime.

4 letters from you yesterday – Hooray – thanks, they do me a
world of good, knowing that you are well. (I have received the
letter with scissors so that I can cut my nails – v.m.t., but I must
have mentioned it before.) Each time the mail comes and is
sorted out there is a feeling of elation and horror – Fred next
door seems to have twice as many as you do, and then Sam has
only 2… So it, I suppose, equals out. How many are you getting
from me – do they all arrive at the same time, or are they arriving
at reasonable intervals? I have no feeling for how long they are
taking – do tell me.

You sound busy. Glad Ciren was fun – a nice break (are your
parents staying with you at all?) and nice to have Toots around.
You sound to be having stacks of mail – why not bundle it all in
one envelope and send it on – or is it too boring in content!

How exciting to be off to London and Kensington Palace next
week.   You'll have forgotten (!) all about it by the time you get
this letter and I look forward to hearing all about it. – Actually, I
wrote him another letter about a week ago, describing a few
things, for he sounded desperate to hear what was going on –
bitter that no-one would tell him!! Fascinating to hear how Wee
goes down and behaves. When is the royal baby due?? About the
same time, I thought… Anyway, I shall be thinking of you –
lucky old thing. Delighted, for it gives you something really

exciting to look forward to. Iain and Liza must have been very impressed to be there that day!

The guess of possible turn round times etc sounds pretty reliable – but I'm not allowed to say and nothing is definite for any ships – to my knowledge. That would be the worst case (and isn't for general discussion!) and could happen (10 days min. leave), but I try to be optimistic and to think that we might be allowed to stay back in good ol' UK. I've got to teach Alfonso a few lessons, now he's woken up!! How I'm longing to see you. Guess it will take some 3 weeks steaming home, once we've set off. A fellow 21 set off yesterday afternoon, so watch out for around 9th July to get idea of timing. So it will have to be an honorary birthday party…

Finances sound a bit grim, but I think the amount going in must have compensated sufficiently. Hope so, and that you have bought yourself and the children exciting presents from me. Is the end of this fiasco in sight? I love you for ever and beyond.   J

HMS Ambuscade.   19/6

Hello Louisa, Hello Marc.
How are you? Daddy is well and looks very strange with a beard, which is now nearly 3 weeks old. I am still wandering around in strange clothes and doing odd things, but I look forward to getting home and changing into my dirty old gardening clothes. How nice it would be to be back with you all, going for walks in the woods and pottering around the garden.

How is Mummy? Are you looking after her and making sure she doesn't work too hard?

Are you both enjoying going to school? Perhaps you can read a little now, Louisa. Have you demolished your school yet, Marc?

I haven't been away for 7 weeks – but it seems much longer. Take great care and look after your precious Mummy. Lots of love to you both from Daddy

20th June
   On screen. (Wind SW, F2, SS3. 288 miles)

HMS Ambuscade.   *Sunday 20*

My darling, Extremely quick – mail going off now by helo to
Hermes. Sunday – not quite quiet, just taking on stores by helo.
Not much happening and don't know future intentions.
   Weather cold, fairly calm, but not too bad. Like a January day
in the channel. Wish I was with you!! I love you, J
   Should I shave off my beard before return?? I think I should
on reaching the Equator! Might frighten the children.

21st June
   On screen, helo ops. 1146 Sunrise. 1930
   Sunset. 2030–2150 RAS(L) RFA TIDESPRING.
   (Wind SW, F2, SS3. 285 miles)

CHAPTER 12

WAITING

A FTER THE SURRENDER of the Argentines came a particularly testing time, because it was not over. Maybe the fighting was, though we could not be absolutely certain even of that, but we dare not let our guard down. We remained for days afterwards in Defence Watches, with our weapons loaded and instantly prepared to fire. We escorted, we patrolled… and we got bored.

After the adrenalin-fired weeks of warfare this continued phase of operations without any perceived threat was very hard to bear. While we needed little to induce the ship's company to keep them alert before, we now had a growing problem.

When would we go home? That was the most frequently asked question around the ship. Rumours were everywhere, and soon some of the ships that had been the first to arrive or had been damaged in battle were released for the long passage home. I remember we went alongside our sister ship, HMS *Arrow*, underway at sea, to transfer to us by jackstay the stores we had run short of. Lucky things, they would no longer need their full array of ammunition and damage control equipment, yet we needed to make up all those items expended. *Arrow* being a chummy ship, there was a degree of pleasant ribaldry passed between the two ships steaming eighty feet apart – but also pangs of jealousy were evident. The shell holes through *Arrow*'s

HMS *Arrow* transferring stores by jackstay
to *Ambuscade* before returning home.

funnel were very obvious scars of her war damage, and a silent reminder of the conflict only just over.

Keeping everyone motivated and on their toes was our biggest challenge, and the mood, as reflected in my letters home, was pretty sombre about the long-term implications to our programme. We understood that we might have to remain there for months ahead. That was then replaced by the rumour that we would be sent home in a matter of weeks, but that after a short period of maintenance we would be required to come back south again, possibly for a deployment of up to nine months. The rumours got more depressing, but there was a most definite feeling that our navy was going to have an awful lot of ships present around the Islands to keep them secure. It was not a pleasant prospect. By this time we were all yearning to see our loved ones back home.

Our routines became tedious and the opportunity to grab morale-boosting activity was scarce. Thankfully, mail became more frequent in that the airfield on the Falklands could now be used, and also fresh ships were arriving.

Westbourne, West Sussex.   *Monday, 21st June, 1982*

My own darling one, Two things this morning – one good (letters from you), and one bad – Princess of Wales has gone into S. Mary's to have her baby. So that scuppers Wednesday's tea, which is rather a blow – it was so nice to have something important in the calendar, which is otherwise fairly bleak until you get home. Fortunately I had been invited out to supper that night, so I have just rung to accept after all – but it is not the same thing!!

I am missing you something 'orrid – Yesterday in church there seemed to be so many husbands around that I felt really in the dumps. However, I was rung up about 11.30 to suggest we all meet at the Good Intent and then have a barbecue lunch together with a bunch of Falklands families. This was really super, and it was a lovely day – but today is wet again and I can't even relieve my frustrations in the garden! It happens to be a totally blank week, which almost never happens – I had thought that London would provide enough excitement. Oh well – at least I've heard from you, which is always a treat, even though it emphasises the distance between us. Your letters were written on 26th and 28th May, nearly a month ago! I long to hear what your 'solo mission' was – in fact, I long to hear all about everything. A doesn't have much to tell (except how Rick Jolly rescued two *Ardent* seamen from a hospital helicopter) and his principal feeling seems to be bitterness that after 11 months of refit, during which he got *Ardent* exactly how he wanted it, she is now at the bottom of the ocean! Also, getting down there after 8,000 miles steaming only to get sunk at once was rather demoralising. I can understand his frustrations. I do adore you, dearest one. Please come back soon. J x

22nd June
On screen. Helo ops. HRH Prince William born. Splice the Mainbrace! (Wind W, F2, SS3. 279 miles)

We spliced the mainbrace in honour of the occasion of the royal birth. The Port Watch Ops Room crew, (off watch) sent a card to St James' Palace with their greetings on the birth of Prince William. Three weeks later, not only did they receive the most courteous (typed) reply, but the Prince of Wales took the trouble to add a personal message of his own at the end in his own handwriting, expressing his admiration and gratitude for our efforts. It meant a great deal to us all at the time.

HMS Ambuscade.   *22/6*

My darlingest one, Tomorrow (no, it's today 25 to 1!) you're meant to be having tea with Prince Charles, but is it still on, the

Royal Birth having taken place yesterday? I wonder… and look forward to hearing all about it if it happens! Hope so, or will you be taken along to hospital, or what? Is there a name for it yet? We Spliced the Mainbrace this evening (what a lot of organisation that meant) – only gave them a third of their allowance – meant to be 3 tots of spirits, but I've said we would save other 2 tots for Sods' Opera on way home, when we can enjoy it. Only half ship's company able to attend first splicing, so we do it again at 0200 – just what I want. Old Chiefs muttering about the disgrace – "Not what it used to be ", and making me annoyed. (I don't think they have seen me annoyed until this evening!)

Seems to be busy still, though life is now boring – no action, no news, same position day in day out. Some prospect of going into the Sound in a few days to rectify a few defects (we're cracking up), which will be a change. Was the Captain's birthday yesterday and I had ship's cartoonist draw him a card, which was signed by all; chefs baked him a cake and we gave him dinner in the wardroom. Good menu laid on, so it meant the Flagship just had to plan a replenishment right in the middle of it. Which meant we had to start at 7 and rush through it at the gallop. Spoilt all the arrangement. First time we have <u>ever</u> RASed at that time of the evening. Typical.

Oh to know when we are returning to where we belong. And oh that we don't have to come rushing back here. I hope that we may get some mail – 5 bags sitting in the FI for us. Also hope that ours may fly out of here in a week or so – this letter may be the first. Certainly it is now being airdropped to FI direct, rather than the 3 week voyage. We may even be able to correspond sensibly. Bliss!

Stay cheerful, my darling, I will be back. Tell the Foreign Secretary to have me returned to look after you all. – or PC. My last letter will arrive in millions of others saying well done, and won't get to him. I won't write to say Congrats, because that would take ages.

I love you passionately. J

Westbourne, West Sussex.   *22nd June, 1982*

Darlingest one, So the world rejoices at the birth of a future king, and probably the only two people in it who are disappointed are Louisa and myself! Ah well, some other time perhaps – and we may then get a glimpse of the new Prince. But it's not the same. Louisa is sad that it's a boy! We'd better have a girl for her sake. Alfonso continues his gentle pressings and twitching – nothing very violent yet, but he is definitely there.

Good news today in the form of a Familygram – I love those, and yours have a definite cachet! I had to look up 'hispid' – and I haven't told Louisa how hairy you are, as that would upset her yet further! It seems that you possibly have had some hints as to your homecoming – familygrams from Antrim a few days ago said "no news", so if you have heard, you're very lucky. I do feel that, dearly though I should love to see you soonest, the Antrim bunch have a higher claim to an early return. But the quicker you all return, the better, and the quicker they tell us when it is likely to be, the happier we shall all be. I wouldn't mind being fobbed off with a totally fictitious programme which was then entirely changed – it's the awful blankness and wild guessing that I hate. People who haven't got husbands away suggest earnestly that one should make one's mind a blank and not listen to any news of rumours but live each day as it comes. Ha ha! They should try it. How can one ignore the whole focus of one's life? Gosh, this sounds bitter, but I don't really feel bitter except at the rain, which is pouring down in torrents and making my plot to pick all the redcurrants totally impracticable – likewise the strawberries, which will rot.

Louisa now has every single waterproof garment she possesses at school – she sets off in one every day, returns without it! Good thing I am collecting her today. I also have to collect some enormous picture. Apparently she has moved on to a New Book, which only 2 of them have got, and she is thrilled. Marc is cutting up a loo roll, so I must drag him off to his club. I love you, my darling. J xxxx

23rd June
   On screen. (Light airs. 306 miles)

24th June
   On screen. Changed to local Time zone (Q)
   retarded clocks 4 hours (28 hour day!).
   Minor relaxation permitted.........chips from
   the deep fat fryer!! (Wind E, light. 365
   miles)

FROM DAILY ORDERS:
   As a follow up to the Captain's sitrep
   this evening, it is intended that a few
   relaxations be made in order to keep up
   our reaction time whilst making life more
   comfortable in Defence Watches. NB
   Relaxations are not compulsory!

a) Anti Flash need not be worn nor trousers
   tucked into socks.

b) Life jackets/Survival suits/AGRs are to be
   taken to your defence watch station. They
   may be left there if you are sent away
   for some reason. Off watch they should be
   readily at hand. Use your common sense and
   take them with you when appropriate.

c) Firesuitmen need not dress up, but must
   check their gear on closing up.

d) NB. You are still required to sleep fully
   dressed and ready to go.

e) Deep fat fryer will be re-commissioned!

HMS Ambuscade.   24/6

My darlingest one, Although nothing is going on, and we just sit well out to sea acting as an escort to the bigger ships, I still seem to be working non-stop. Which is not a bad thing for it would be very boring otherwise (and is, nevertheless!). No mail for quite a time now, though I understand there are 6 bags ashore for us. Hopefully this letter will be flown out by the end of the month, so should be with you faster than usual. <u>Did</u> you go to Kensington Palace for tea, or was it all cancelled or postponed? Longing to hear all.

My day yesterday: up at 0645, breakfast, read the signals and action various ones. Brief various people on day's activities, do some paperwork, attend a Mid's talk to some of the ship's coy., debrief him, mark some test books, attend Captain's requestmen table, 20 min. lunch, read / action more signals, attend other Mid's talk and debrief him, 3 hours or so with Captain, discussing morale of ship's coy. and my plans for upping it, 3½ hour meeting with other HODs (Heads of Departments), quiet supper, 1 hour writing daily orders, 1 hour discussing improvements to weapon systems of Type 21s to be included when we return, then more paperwork, then 1½ hours with Captain discussing his collision report and telling him what I thought he should write. (We collided with a tanker during our first RAS down here, nothing too bent, and no-one hurt, but I didn't mention it at the time – didn't want to worry you or spread malicious rumours…!) Then wandered around ship (about 0100 by now), had sardines on toast at 0130, few more signals etc. and then in bed just after 02.

Today we are putting the clocks back from 1200 to 0800 – a massive time jump which will do odd things to our body clocks and give us 2 watches! So we will be working a 28-hour day, for a change!

My main consideration at the moment is holding the ship's coy. together in the period of quasi-war. We have to remain closed up and ready in all respects, but nothing is happening and they are seriously bored and have nothing concrete to look forward to. Even if they knew our return date was December, it would be better because it would seem real. Minor irritants have become exaggerated and I am doing my utmost to get rid of them and keep the whole thing ticking over. Quite a task, for it spreads from officers downwards and there is little to do to correct it. I hope we will be allowed to see the Islands and meet the people before too long – that would help.

Meanwhile, I long to hear from you and even more to be with you. It can't be too long from now… Take the greatest care. Give my love to the children. I love you, you mean everything to me. J

Westbourne, West Sussex.   *Thursday, 24th June*
                              (on a larger free airmail form)

My dearest one, What a smart big form we have! Westbourne Post Office has obviously got them in specially for me…

I feel very spoilt this week, with lots of letters and a family gram from you. I long to know if the 'hopeful horoscopes' and honeymoons and homecomings mean that you have actually got a date, even if it is only provisional? I should love to think that you have, as it makes it all real. *Alacrity* got back today, only because her gun barrel needed replacing. Come on, fight harder!!

It was lovely to hear how you spend your day, and what you wear and so on. Louisa is appalled to hear that you sleep in all your kit – "But his sheets will get all dirty and he hasn't got a washing machine!"

Our big news of course is that we did go to Kensington Palace yesterday for tea. I rang PC on Tuesday at about 4 to say we won't come (got straight through on a private line, but it turns out that it also belongs to a Kensington hotel, and there were some hilarious scenes when we were there, with people trying to book rooms…), and he insisted that we should go. So we left Marc with Iain and Liza and went off with beautiful hair and well-pressed clothes – Lady Sarah A-J showed us where to go, as the Palace is a <u>mass</u> of doors, and we were welcomed in and taken over by the equerry. We had tea with him, as it turned out that someone had come to see PC on business – due at 4.00, but arrived late at 4.15, and we were a few minutes early at 4.25. Anyway, we went in at 5.00, and saw the apartment – not big, not grand, but very nice. Then upstairs to the nursery, where Prince ??? was being dressed. Apparently it will not be a traditional name, but they both have definite ideas. Anyway, PC took him downstairs when he was ready, and he certainly seemed to know his father already. Louisa was too shy to brush the royal hair – not much of it, but it was a <u>most</u> enchanting baby. Louisa was given a sweet little china Bilson box from Aspreys with a mouse from 'The Tailor of Gloucester' on the top. She is going to keep her silver cross in it. Bit more chat and we left at 5.55, very well satisfied. An hour to the McNeil's, where Marc was fed, bathed and ready for bed, and Jerbs fed and walked. Wee played with Claire and got ready for bed, and we came home exhausted. Iain wants to see you and hear all about it. So do I! Love J x

25th June
    On screen. Drills and exercises. Helo ops. Ambuscade is informed she will return to UK "after 28 July". (Wind E, F4, SS3. 300 miles)

HMS Ambuscade.   *25/6*

Darlingest J, another quiet day on the screen with no activity and just general work onboard. We shall have a film tonight – *The Deep* – same producer as *Jaws*.

My letter of yesterday – optimism may be just a little more than wishful thinking, according to something in today. <u>But</u> all programmes are subject to change and <u>highly</u> classified, so not a word to a soul about my guess – keep it <u>very</u> much to yourself (completely, in fact – I'd be shot!). Can't remember exactly what I said, but I am going around with a smile on my (inner) face. Ship's company and officers know nothing as yet. Official word will be some time in coming, so if you hear nothing for a while, don't worry at all. No word of this…!

Darlingest, I love you and long for you, more than you can guess. What bliss it will be to be back with you and we must head off for a holiday as soon as possible – I hope Wales will be OK (hope for 2 weeks' leave, very shortly after arrival) – again, not a word. How exciting, but dates you won't learn for another couple of weeks. Mr. Vernon did say the shorter the notice, the better, didn't he!!

Of course I don't know what your plans are at all – perhaps you've booked it at some other time. However, difficult as it is, we must fix something. Perhaps a week at home and a week in Wales. I love you – keep smiling. All my love, J

Another!   25/6

Darlingest J, Mail at long last and this one to you will go off at 06 tomorrow and <u>fly</u> out. Hooray, at long last perhaps we may correspond without 6 weeks going by. 2 letters from you (including the pressed flowers, for which many thanks – v. good!). As always, fabulous to hear from you and that you sound much happier now that all seems over. It's more of a relief to you than us, for firstly you can celebrate and we can't (half a pint this evening and most eves) , and secondly we have to wait out here just in case they care to attack us.

Letters also from my ma (with 3 snaps which is nice, do thank her, I'll write sometime…), from your ma (tell her about the free airmails!) and from Prince Charles – another long letter dated 13th just to say he'd rung you up and was still anxious.   Hadn't received my second letter, but was looking forward to seeing you and Wee for tea "with us", but did it happen…? Longing to hear all. He said he was near Portsmouth and nearly popped in to see you!

Anyway – awful day for us – we suddenly put the clocks back 4 hrs so it is really now 01 in body time although the clock tells one it's 2100. I must away to bed, for I'm tired.

I hear from my ma she has been left a legacy which she's spending on her back treatment – is she still suffering from that and is treatment working?

I'm glad to hear your Pa is back to his normal self and that they will be with you for some of July. Wish I could be... But you never know, one day they are going to turn round and say Head North, and we will say Aye Aye! I've nothing to base it on but have a slight feeling it could be end of July / early August – but don't believe that – better to believe 'autumn'. Fingers crossed and don't breathe a word as rumours are terrible things and, founded as this one is on nothing, can do no good! It's my will-power working overtime, trying to get us home to where we belong.

I _must_ try to write to the children, but I haven't really anything to describe to them, it's all so alien and different. How are they?

Write, write, write to me! Love, love love. All of it, and there's an enormous amount. J

Westbourne, West Sussex.   *Friday 25th June, 1982*

My darlingest one, Yet more letters today – I feel very spoilt! That's some every day except Thursday. I only hope that you are also getting lots – Caroline and I both feel thoroughly annoyed that our letters don't seem to be getting through!

I am watching a film of the taking of Port Stanley. It's all fascinating, and I hope you get a chance to see what was happening ashore. But we still don't know exactly what _you_ and the other ships were up to, and I hope that at some stage we shall have a run-down of your activities. However, the ITV film crew are home tonight, so it seems that reporting on the Falklands is at an end. At least I can now stop goggling – the 9 o'clock and 10

The author, bearded (centre) on the bridge
in beret and foul weather gear.

o'clock news each night has been hard watching! I think Alfonso will probably be a politician – papers, the *Economist* and the TV and radio news have been my mental diet recently. I'd better start on something more cultural quickly!

We have all been so exhausted by the last few days that we didn't wake up till 8 today, and I had to shake the children. Marc had his Teddy Bears' Picnic at playschool in the pouring rain, so they had it all indoors. He was too shy to race well, though I am told he usually wins. I left him to paint teddies and went home to have a good session in the attic, which was useful. He had lunch at school, and was thrilled to have chips! Told everyone about it. Things I didn't tell you about Wednesday's trip, as I ran out of space – Wee wore her Wedding dress, so it did get to go to the party after all! We took as a present the Hide and Seek Alphabet book, which went down very successfully, I'm glad to say. Louisa wrote a label to go with it, and he tucked it inside the book to keep. Louisa was rather shy, but impressed him by correctly naming various animals in pictures he had around,

26/6

Dear Louisa and Marc,

Guess what, it's 6 o'clock in the evening on Saturday night — pitch darkness outside, so they have told us to steam alongside another, bigger, ship to take on some petrol from it. Just what I want to spend my Saturday evening doing, especially as I had organised the rest of the officers to sit down together for dinner. This seems to have happened before this week .....

What we do is this, steam up to the other ship, shoot a line across & haul across a big hose to pump the fuel through. It all takes about 2 hours which means our supper including a magpie. She bounced about a bit on the carpet with Fat Dolly (also in the dress I made for the wedding), but was never at all out of hand or obtrusive – just lacking toys!

How I long for your return! But take great care in the meantime. It's lovely to hear we are rich, though it's more on paper than in reality...

Darling one, I just want you home again to share our lives. I love you. J x

26th June
    On screen. 2000-2100 RAS(L) HMS BAYLEAF.
    Depart for San Carlos waters for repairs.
    (Wind E, F4, SS2. 304 miles)

HMS Ambuscade.   *26/6*

Dear Louisa and Marc, Guess what, it's 6 o'clock in the evening on Saturday night – pitch darkness outside, so they have told us to steam alongside another, bigger ship to take on some petrol from it. Just what I want to spend my Saturday evening doing, especially as I had organised the rest of the officers to sit down together for dinner. This seems to have happened before this week...

What we do is this: steam up to the other ship, shoot a line across and haul across a big hose to pump the fuel through. It all takes about 2 hours, which means my supper will be spoilt.

How are you both? Enjoying lots of parties, school, picnics, gardens, pools, visits, ice-creams and lollipops (?). Thank you Marc for your lovely picture. Can I have some more from both of you, please?

Hope to see you quite soon. I'll shave my beard off first. Look after Mummy. Lots of love, Daddy

HMS Ambuscade.   *26/6*

My darlingest, 6 letters, (including a card) and a postcard have poured into the ship today. First ones to arrive dated 21st, and last dated 4th June!! So rather confusing and I think there must be some more on its way to fill in a gap or two. Lovely, as ever, to hear your news and that you are well (sorry about Louisa's sunstroke, no doubt she's over that – and what are these stitches Marc had out?? Hadn't heard of this!)

We aren't censored, but we do have to keep to the censorship rules, hence my reluctance occasionally! Especially now, when all are smiling with Good News, yet we aren't allowed to write home about it. Nor will we for another couple of weeks. I'm sure PM abides strictly by the rules, so it would be disastrous if even any feelings get out! But letters will dry up for a while soon, so…

How exciting: good news, lots of mail – people are actually smiling – terrible, I must see what I can do about it. We have blank days for 12 days now and don't complain, although monotony is there and we have to keep our guard up lest some crazy Argies decide to get going again. So we remain closed up and ready for anything.

Hope to steam in overnight to the Falklands and Bomb Alley (but no bombs, I hope) for a couple of days. Will be interesting to see what they look like – have only seen them in moonlight and being illuminated by starshell.

Points from your letter: gannex rug – in shed on top of tea chests??? Porch – I'll draw in another letter: how are our finances? £565 is the amount being paid in at the end of the month (any day) – which I wrote to tell you about some 4 weeks ago. Not too bad and should sort us out, hopefully. Have you bought yourself a Jaeger outfit for Kensington Palace??? Presumably that never came off, but you never know; did it?)

Glad you've got away to the theatre, etc., sounds good and you haven't fainted – well done! Hope Alfonso is cheering up these days – I've got a thing or two to show him before too long!!

Ambuscade alongside *Stena Seaspread*
in San Carlos.

The garden sounds magnificent. I look forward to tasting the products…

All my love to you, precious one. J

27th June
Berthed alongside MV STENA SEASPREAD at anchor. (Wind E, F4, SS1. 250 miles)

HMS Ambuscade. 27/6

My darlingest J, Just before midnight and we are tucked up alongside another ship in San Carlos water, where the landings first took place. 'Bomb Alley' – but I trust not now. However, we take no chances and remain fully closed up ready to go. Had a couple of scares in the last 24 hours, but nothing materialised. This could be the last letter for some few days, because opportunities to land mail will be non-existent, but then you will get another batch all at once. Do keep writing because the same will happen in reverse. After that point, don't write!!

All is well, and people are relieved. However, we have work to do first and will be kept busy. Longing to see you and hear all about everything. How are the strawberries and the peas etc. etc. I love your card of the garden flowers – thank you very much – what a lot we have and what a clever girl I'm married to. I was clever too, to find you!

My sweetest, I 'm off to bed: I've now got quite a lot of photos surrounding me of you and the family – from both parents.

Keep smiling and do so more and more. I love you and will show you that soon. (Don't give the game away until it is confirmed officially.) Love to the children, but all to you. (beard comes off soon…) J

27/6

Dear Louisa and Marc, Firstly here are two hairs from Daddy's beard! – a white one which had to come out – the only white one,

I may say, and another black one just to show you that I have some.

There are icebergs down here, but I haven't seen any. Big lumps of ice, much bigger than my ship. They float on the sea like islands.

I have seen some funny black ducks today: just like this drawing!

Ambuscade dwarfed by *Stena Seaspread*.

Otherwise there is a lot of kelp – which is seaweed and floats on the surface of the water. And the ubiquitous (look it up) seagull.

There are sheep ashore, with thick coats for the winter. But it's not too cold for us, and I haven't got frostbite.

Lots of love, Daddy

28th June
   Alongside. Hot debate on method for hull crack repairs.

Westbourne, West Sussex.   *Monday, 28th June, 1982*

Darlingest one, It seems that Sarah had a telegram from Peter over the period of her father's death last week, in which he'd said "Be back soon to help" – so we're all wondering if it means what it says! Anyway, it all sounds quite hopeful, though I was told yesterday that the latest plot was for at least 9 frigates and destroyers to stay there for a year, working shifts of 15 weeks – 3 weeks down, 6 weeks on station, 3weeks back, 3 weeks leave. Ah well. Naturally we all speculate madly all the time, but place no faith in our speculations. I've put on some Boots Best Bitter just in case – the barrel won't last very long after you return!

Pause to investigate Bee's sudden silence: he is standing in a corner of the drawing-room with some pens in his hand and looking v. guilty, though I can't see anything wicked that he's done. Perhaps he is just contemplating it – I've just been told to "Get out from us home!" We are out to coffee shortly; had lunch out on Saturday and went to the Donkey Derby with your mother on Sunday. This consisted of fairground rides, displays by the TS band and the Chichester Twirlettes (!) and some very young Morris dancers; races by reluctant donkeys and inept jockeys, and candy floss and popcorn.

I have decided that the children's present can be an electric toothbrush! They cost about £10, but I am sure it will help them brush their teeth a lot better. We still seem to be getting through our money jolly fast, which is disappointing. Help, no space – I love you madly but can't say so 'cause I've run out of letter! Jx

28th June, 1982

Darling one, I ran out of space this morning, and couldn't tell you how much I love you. I do look forward to demonstrating it when you return – I am planning a delicious dinner of hot tongue and mushy peas and Cadbury's Smash [*least favourite foods!*]. Actually you are going to be Too Late for the soft fruit, which is bad luck – we have stuffed ourselves nightly and given quite a bit away, but I have still made enough jam, and frozen enough puree to last us the year. We have had quite a good crop of raspberries too – enough for me to enjoy each night! The first sweet peas are now in the house and the dahlia buds are swelling. But my favourite dahlia is defunct, alas! I shall have to get another next year. My lilies are coming on nicely, and I have a little row of mesembryanthemums just for you! Fancy being able to spell mes… just after bottling the Vinamat Vermouth. It shows I didn't swallow too much!

I had a letter from someone in Vernon today – they are getting together the Portsmouth area wives of *Brilliant, Broadsword, Ambuscade, Active* and *Danae*. There's an entertainer for the children and coffee for the mums on 6th July, and I am looking forward to it. There can't be too many of us, as it seems from the odd mistake that it is an individually typed and signed letter. Jolly nice of them – though obviously none of you will be anywhere near home by then, which seems a bit hard on the *Brilliant* and *Broadsword* lot – they've worked jolly hard for a long time, haven't they? – Not, she adds hastily, that you haven't too!

Darling one, the summer has turned sour, and I want you home to cheer it up – blow away the rain and wind with a huge unending kiss. For heaven's sake don't go for a stroll among the mines round Port Stanley, and tie yourself carefully on each time you go on deck. You are so <u>very</u> precious to me, and Alfonso is longing to meet you. I've started reading books on the Antarctic. I love you. J x

CHAPTER 13

NEW ORDERS

29th June

>   Alongside. Weld cracks. Fuel from MV ANCO
>   CHARGER at anchor. Receive orders to
>   escort MV St EDMUND to Ascension with High
>   Risk Prisoners of War.

Alongside tanker in San Carlos waters. A Type 42 Destroyer
is passing by with a Sea King Helicopter flying above.

HMS Ambuscade.   *29/6 San Carlos Water*

My dearest darling, I thought my last letter would be the last for a while, but here is another! We are now alongside a tanker taking on fuel whilst at anchor in S Carlos – where *Antelope* sank and the landings took place. No move quite yet.

No mail for a few days now, hope we get some before…

The Islands look just like Mull – bleak, low cloud, occasional snow, squalls and even a penguin looking a bit lost! Boats (our rubber one) take the gash ashore to burn and come back with bags of FI heather, which we are then going to sell at 10p a sprig at a Country Fair – to raise money for FI fund and our welfare fund. Someone has got a bucket of soil to put in a tray so others can spend 10p to tread on FI soil – and then we will sell it off to them! So we hope we can relax a bit eventually – but first we have a smally task to do.

Won't it be lovely to <u>talk</u> to each other! Longing for our reunion – what fun!

Take great care and don't do too much. I want to come back to a scruffy house, grass 3 feet deep and weeds all over the place. Then I'll know that you have been looking after yourself! All my love to you and love to children. J

30th June
    Alongside. Flying operations. 2230 sail, escorting St EDMUND. (15 miles)

During this period in San Carlos, our helicopter flew to the place that HMS *Ardent* was sunk, and dispatched a wreath from the helicopter made up from welding rods for the frame and covered in moss and heather that we had collected from ashore in San Carlos. A typical gesture of solidarity from the Type Twenty One Club.

Westbourne, West Sussex.   *Wednesday 30th June, 1982*

My dearest one, Stacks of letters from you this morning – a real treat, especially since the last one was written on 26th June! As you say, a real correspondence now seems possible – though it doesn't sound as though you have had anything like all my letters. I hope they're not all at the bottom of the sea somewhere.

Sarah rang yesterday to suggest that we should think in terms of the end of July – frightfully exciting! As you say, even if it was December it would be all right – just having something to focus on is what one needs. And if it really is at the end of the month – well!! We shall have to clean the house and weed the garden and chuck out all the marijuana we've been growing so successfully, together with all the hippie folk and their 26 cats…

What can I tell you? Neighbour has a smart new car. We are hoping to win £500 in the church raffle. We <u>didn't</u> go to Butlins in Bognor with the Mothers and Toddlers, which was just as well in view of the rain. I have sanded down and varnished the children's bunks, which is a great improvement. It has been too wet to paint the windows. I have bought the children's electric toothbrush, but thought I would keep it for you to give them – you won't have much in the way of souvenirs from the

Falklands! I have also bought myself a present, as per order from you – it is a hair styling thing which the hairdresser used before I went to Kensington Palace, and it is magically effective. Hope you like the result! All of which is Awfully Extravagant, and I hope we have something in the a/c when you get home… Gosh, it will be wonderful – but I do want you to come <u>home</u> and not have to stay in Plymouth. It's just not the same at all, but I realise that someone will have to stay with the ship. I do adore you so much, and long to have you here. It all sounds pretty boring out there – but I love you, don't forget. J x

1st July
    Passage to Port Stanley. 1555 sunset.
    Remain in vicinity of Port Stanley.
    Captain reports atmosphere too relaxed to
    remain properly alert. Disappointment
    onboard that further delays to our
    departure have arisen. Difficulties on
    political side with MV St EDMUND delay
    sailing to at least 5th July. (Wind SW,
    F4,SS3. 250 miles)

Approaching Fort Stanley. Type 21 Frigate and Landing Craft ahead with Wessex Helicopter overhead.

HMS Ambuscade.   *Still off FI 1/7*

Darlingest J, Still here, flogging up and down the coast at slow speed waiting for someone to tell us what to do. But no news. Meanwhile no mail, no action, no interest. Bad news, our hopes having been raised and then just kept hanging around.

It snowed yesterday, and I saw a penguin (just like the wind-up ones we have in the bath!). I went onboard a British Rail ferry to inspect it with regard to a future duty of ours. Those ferries will never be the same to me; this one has been a prison ship.

As you can see, we are Bored and Impatient. We have tried sending a few signals as hints but no results as yet. All thoroughly boring boring boring!

I hope this finds you in a better frame of mind, and that all is well. Hopefully all this won't delay us too long, and all our optimism remains high. Every hour down here now is wasted.

Meanwhile, days seem to be long because of various activities. We still sleep fully dressed and carry funny things around with us, and work watch on / watch off / watch on / watch off. It hasn't helped to find out that our Captain F is back in 'cruising watches' i.e. 1 in 4 rather than 1 in 2, and having a comparative ball, only a few miles from us. Ship's coy. know it and don't like the difference – neither do I, but I can't change it, nor perhaps should I.

Meanwhile, as ever, not a word to anyone. I love you and long for you and will be with you before not too long (though ½ hour is too long!). J

Westbourne, West Sussex.   *1st July*

Happy Lunaversary, my darling! And just as Marc started getting going on the kicking routine on 1st May 3 years ago, so Alfonso has really woken up in a big way, and told me he didn't want to go to sleep last night! Isn't it fun?

I have been dashing around with a paint brush doing

windowsills and skirting boards and boring such-like things – only inside, alas, as it is again raining after a nice day yesterday when I got the grass cut. Then suddenly the postman stuck his head around the door with two more super letters from you – 19th & 20th June, which means that they got lost somewhere for a while. Nice, as I love getting mail little and often, but it usually arrives in a heap, and I couldn't possibly wait a day to open some of it!

We are about to lunch with Charlotte and post our electric blanket to be serviced – Aren't I good?! So is Marc, actually – after him sitting down in some paint & leaning on some more, some ducks turned up to be fed, so he went off to do that, and has been quietly entertaining himself ever since. I shall go and play with him now.

Wee breaks up on 9 July, and my parents come to stay on 12th until Saturday. Then I shall start making preparations for you!! Even if you don't come, I shall still enjoy it. I do love you so much. Enclosed one boring list of promotions – I know you have a signal but I thought you'd like to see it. All my love Jx

2nd July.
> Rejoined CBG at first light. Screening station. Vertrep with RFA FORT GRANGE. 2100 Anti submarine exercise overnight! Ordered to embark 60 Scots Guards to transport to South Georgia to relieve M Company Royal Marines, who had recaptured the island on 25th April. (Wind SW, F5,SS4. 326 miles)

FROM DAILY ORDERS:
> Beard growing competition. Don't shave off your set.
> A grand beard growing competition will be

```
held at Lat 20 South (about a week after
sailing north). Prizes will be given for
the following categories:
i) Longest individual hair
ii) "Fullest" set
Iii) Most pathetic natural effort
Iv) The most artistic and original cut.
```

CHANGED ORDERS

After what seemed an eternity, our orders came through to transport a company of the Scots Guards to South Georgia to relieve the Royal Marines who had recaptured it at the very beginning of the war. This was a challenge in itself, for to take a 40 strong group of men, plus equipment, on a passage into Antarctic waters required a lot of thought and effort as to how to shoe-horn them in. Pretty much every office, store room, sonar space, nook, cranny and even the mast housed our army guests. The army has always been known affectionately to the Navy as Pongos, and although there is always friendly rivalry between the different services, it was fun to have a new task and to meet new friends. We had much to discuss with them to get to understand what had been going on in each others' very different war. Morale, which had undeniably dropped away with all the uncertainties of the future programme and the boredom of relative inaction, picked up again, though our thoughts were inevitably on when we might be returning home.

Westbourne, West Sussex.   *2nd July*

Dearest darlingest loveliest absentee,
I am lolling in bed watching the news with one eye while I write to you – Evidently SDP card-carriers don't read either *The Economist* or *The Sunday Times*, as they have just elected Roy

Jenkins. Not that it matters anyway – Maggie still seems to be riding high in popularity, and no-one is much interested in other parties; though with all the strikes deluging upon us, things may change.

Now I'm watching *"Falklands Diary"* – Jeremy Hands and Michael Nicholson describing their experiences and so on. Michael N has just said that the *Atlantic Conveyor* was hit after the Exocet had been deflected by chaff – the first time anyone has said that she was hit via another ship – it's always been said that the Argentines thought she was *Hermes* or *Invincible*. They (ITV) have made a video cassette called *"Battle for the Falklands"* – it will be interesting to see how well it sells. Strange, the fascination of war.

I have spent the day painting again – I've top coated the inside of our bedroom windows and now only have to remove the marks left by the masking tape. I've also been touching up skirting boards and other yellowing paint – it all looks so much better and brighter, but it has made the not-done bits look even worse, and there seem to be so many of them once one starts looking! Marc doesn't exactly help – he came home from playschool and promptly jumped on the newly-painted drawing room windowsill – which now says "Superkids" in mirror writing over half of it!

3rd July

Fell asleep over the end of the programme – had a rotten night, and find I have a cold and sore throat this morning, which is very bad luck. Marc had a slight cold recently, so I guess I got it from him. We're all feeling unenthusiastic about life, but Wee is quietly drawing and Marc is playing with his Teddy Bear mask from the teddy bears' picnic at school, so at least life is fairly gentle.

Your Ma came in yesterday, on the way to Barnstaple for Nathaniel's christening on Sunday. I couldn't find anything to send, so am asking what they want – though Lain's has a pretty pair of decanters for £30 – possible wedding present for Stephen if we have any money at the time!

I shall go and dig up some french bean plants for Susan – we have too many in one row, and there is nowhere to plant extras out! Had first courgettes last night – frightfully disappointing to find that three of them had rotted half-way down in the rain. But at least yesterday was hot and today is fine. We all send heaps and heaps of love, and long to see you. Jx

3rd July
   Anti submarine exercise until 0600. Helo ops to vertrep extra stores (food and camp beds) for troops' passage to South Georgia. 1000-1055 RAS(L) with RFA TIDEPOOL, then detached to Port Stanley. 2000 FALL OUT FROM DEFENCE WATCHES. Now in Cruising Watches of 4 hours length. (Wind W, F4, SS5. 305 miles)

4th July
   0759 Sunrise. 0800 Enter Port Stanley and anchor. Embark 40 members of 2nd Battalion Scots Guards. 1330 Sail to CBG to pick up personnel. 1553 Sunset. (Wind SW, F4,SS2. 231 miles)

HMS Ambuscade.   *Off FI 4/7*

Darlingest J, I think it's the 4th, but I can't find my diary!

We sneaked away from the Falkland Islands hoping that it would prompt someone into doing something about us and we've been given another job. Spent last 24 hours topping up with stores and fuel (pretty rough and driving blizzards to keep us in seasonal feelings) and are now heading back into Stanley to collect a mass of Pongos to transport to another unmentionable island before our long haul northwards. All, as ever, not allowed to be talked about, but hope to see you within my birthday month. What a lovely thought, but don't go around with a large grin on your face lest someone guesses. We will be allowed to communicate officially in something like 2 weeks' time. This is positively my last letter for that sort of time. Still none from you – it's all been diverted to an island in the sun. We just haven't caught up with it yet!

A new admiral has taken over. Otherwise, what news? Little to report. It's been a boring few weeks, with long hours but no meat. (The food, actually, continues to be pretty good and I think I'm putting on weight again.)

I've suddenly realised my birthday mail will be some 10 days delayed. What a tragedy!

How are the children – give them a big kiss from me and tell them I'll be home to play with them soon. And with you...!! Longing to see you and be with you again. May these next few weeks speed past. All my love to you, my darlingest J. Not long now, and then another honeymoon. J

Midnight 4th

Darlingest, A helo delivering a new Head of Department to us is on its way and may take back mail to the battle group, and that could find its way to FI and to you. So, a quick note to say that I love you. We are heading towards icebergs and penguins with pongos onboard, but then will shave off ready...

Getting away from here is a lovely feeling, but still lots to do.

Snowed hard today and we have white decks.

Longing to see you. Take care. All my love to you J

Westbourne, West Sussex.   *American Independence Day*

What ho my darling, Stars for ever, but you can keep the stripes. Put some on Alfonso.

I think I should warn you about the Bump, which is suddenly very manifest. Fatty Mrs Lippy. Do you think you can still love

such an unsympathetic heap of blubber? Talking of blubber, I am reading *South Latitude* – all about the whaling station on South Georgia which I imagine sparked the war. It's very interesting.

Darling, can you possibly let me know what is likely to happen when you get home? I imagine PM will go off on leave immediately, but does this mean you ought to stay on board and take second leave? If I knew what the situation was likely to be, I could perhaps arrange something when I get that blissful call from the Ministry. The children, at least Louisa, with an echo from Marc – are greatly looking forward to your return. Louisa said today "Will you be happy when Daddy gets back?" which makes me feel I must have been a Glum Mum! Actually I have been this weekend, as I have had a perfectly foul cold and sore throat that have reduced me to a rotten heap. Louisa has been magnificent, and has taken Marc off my hands entirely. For instance, when he wanted me to push him in his swing, she said "No, I will push you", and was simply sweet with him for hour after hour. Anyway, we went to have tea with the Parsons this afternoon, as I felt that they should have a romp with other children, and after that I began to feel better. I went to bed very early last night, and expect to be fine tomorrow. Fortunately there are some magnificent old films being shown on TV at the moment, and I watched Fassbender's *Despair* last night, and *Death in Venice* tonight. They go on all week, plus two Noel Coward plays – I really don't see how I am to get any sewing done at all! And we go to Bernard d'Ascoli on Thursday. I am taking Bim and Susan, which should be super.

The garden has started to produce – our first courgettes, potatoes, french beans, carrots and blackcurrants have been consumed, and there are still rasps and strawbs and redcurrants and peas and broad beans going strong. It's all rather overwhelming, but pretty much under control.

Both mothers thank you for your letters, and my ma has passed on to Francis Pym your kind words about the govt. support. He was very concerned to know about mail getting through – Hear Hear! Let's have a free telephone link installed. How I long to hear your voice! My darling one, take every care and remember how terribly precious you are to me. Come back soon! J x

5th July
     0047 left TEZ after 44 days. 0100 Helo
     transfer of personnel Passage to South
     Georgia. 0734 Sunrise. Starboard Tyne main
     engine air intakes frozen up. 1515 Sunset.
     (Wind SW, F7 near gale, SS4. 326 miles)

FROM DAILY ORDERS:
     UPPER DECK. Conditions on the upper deck
     will get progressively worse as we approach
     South Georgia's snow, ice and roughers. The
     upper deck will remain out of bounds and
     there will be no lifebuoy sentry closed up.
     EXCEPTIONS: In daylight personnel wishing
     to get some fresh air may seek the
     permission of the Officer of the Watch to

Heavy weather on passage to South Georgia.

proceed onto the boat deck. Upper deck
rounds will be carried out as directed
by OOW.

Westbourne, West Sussex.   *5th July, 1982*

Darlingest one, The children both went to sleep this afternoon, so they didn't settle till after nine – then I was cooking for a lunch on Wed. with SM and J, so time has flown right away. I go to coffee at HMS *Vernon* tomorrow, followed by lunch with JH, so that's the whole day gone, dammit. I'm really getting my teeth into painting – it's far from beautiful and elegant, but may keep some of the condensation at bay next winter.

Darling, two more letters today sounding V. hopeful, esq.!! Actually, word has already reached me via Sarah, who has some extremely useful contacts. And she has told me quite a lot that I am surprised that she knew about – I have been soft-pedalling my info. and saying little, but you needn't worry too much about breaking censorship rules or telling me things you aren't quite sure I ought to know. Anyway, I hope more letters do arrive. It sounds as though we shall be starved for a while.

Sleepy time is upon me – wish you were here to share it.

I do adore you – and we had an antenatal check this morning, and Alfonso adores you too. J x

6th July
>   Passage. Warning of icebergs in area. Port
>   Olympus main engine intake frozen up.
>   (Wind W, F8-9 gale, SS4-6 very rough. 322
>   miles)

Westbourne, West Sussex.   *Tuesday 6th July*

Darling one, Yet more mail this a.m., which is simply lovely – it all sounds v. exciting, and I am <u>thrilled</u> for you to have seen a whole penguin! Bring back a tail feather for me.

Went to HMS *Vernon* this morning for our wives' coffee – only about 6 *Ambuscade*, but we did better than most of the ships! It was all "I'm Liz / Carol / Linda" and so on, and I didn't like to ask anyone what their husbands did in case they asked about mine. When they discovered Sarah was the captain's wife at the end, they were appalled – "Ooh, I'm so sorry!". So we primly ate sausage rolls and salmon sandwiches and a chap plugged away at a guitar trying to get the children to sing, but it was all most peculiar, and I think the spirit of the crisis was over. *Active* is evidently on her way back, or nearly so, judging by what the wife of the PWO said – what fun if you came together!

Bad news of the day was that the parents were rammed from behind while taking Isolde on a trip – Ma was thrown out and had to have stitches, leaving Daddy to cope with Isolde! All rather grim but not too serious, except that the car is likely to be

The piper on the bridge roof entering
Grytviken Harbour 7 July.

a write-off and even though the other chap is to blame it is bound to cost them money. And Daddy is scared to drive. Bim fetches them next weekend to stay here, and I will take them back next. Then we shall return to await orders! All my love, dearest one. J x

SOUTH GEORGIA

A most memorable day was *Ambuscade*'s entrance into Grytvicken Harbour in South Georgia. This was where the first engagements were with the scrap dealers who had started the conflict some six months before. We sailed past icebergs, lit by the sunlight to give an incredible blue tint, and rounded the inlet into the harbour to see the scarlet-hulled HMS *Endurance* alongside. (She was the Antarctic guardship which had been our only presence down in the South Atlantic before the war. She was affectionally known in the RN as the "Red Plum" on account of her colour).

I had stationed a piper from the Scots Guards on top of the bridge roof to pipe us into harbour. I recall he was not too effective, and I shouted up, "Come on, Pipes, play some more!" to which he replied, "I can't, sir, I canna move me fingers!" The bitter cold had taken its toll.

It was also a significant day for me – 7th July, 1982, and my 33rd birthday! For the first time since leaving Ascension Island, we had some social activity and went onboard *Endurance* for a very jolly lunch.

That afternoon we walked across to the deserted but rather romantic ruins of the erstwhile whaling station, tucked under the high, snow-clad mountains that once had been scaled by Ernest Shackleton, a hero of mine. Alongside a jetty there was another reminder of the war: the Argentine submarine *Santa Fe*, which had been attacked by Royal Navy helicopters and sunk. We subsequently learnt much more about the operations in South Georgia and the excitements of M Company, Royal Marines, who had fought to retake the islands; their story stirred the heart.

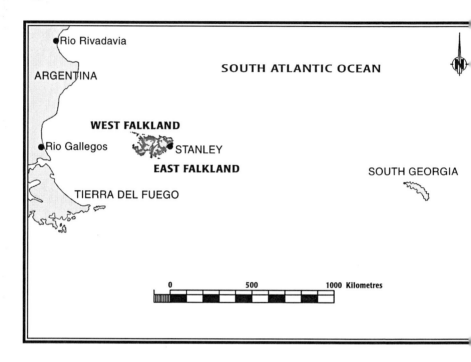

7th July

Enter Grytviken harbour, South Georgia just after dawn. Berth alongside MV SCOTTISH EAGLE, fuel. Land Scots Guards, embark 40 personnel of M Company Royal Marines. 1433 Slip and proceed. Passage to Ascension Island. Navigating past icebergs. (Wind S, F2, SS2)

8th July

Passage north, negotiating icebergs. (Wind S, F2, SS2. 397 miles)

Chipping the ice off the 4.5 inch Gun.

Abandoned old whalers in Grytviken.

HMS *Endurance*,
South Georgia.

Ambuscade in South Georgia
alongside tanker.

Grytviken Whaling Station.

Giant iceberg, on passage from
South Georgia.

CHAPTER 14

BACK
TO ASCENSION

W E HAD AT one stage expected to transport M Company back to the Falkland Islands, but welcome news came with instructions that we were to take them 4,000 miles north to Ascension Island, from where they would all be flown home. At last we were moving in a homewards direction, though we had every expectation that, once back in the UK, we would be rapidly turned around to return to the Falkland Islands. The uncertainty of the future certainly didn't stop us from enjoying the prospect of homecoming and we sought to relax just a bit, getting the ship and ourselves gradually back to some semblance of normality. We reduced the damage control state to open up doors and hatches, securing the Damage Control Parties and stowing away their equipment. All the weapons and sensors were however kept at full readiness, and our guard was still kept high. The state of the peace seemed to us somewhat fragile. It wasn't all plain sailing either. We were still in southern waters and encountered some frightful weather conditions as we steamed north. It was far from comfy and we continued to fear for the safety of the ship. The welded-up cracks in the hull ominously started opening up again.

```
SIGNAL RECEIVED 080839Z
   TO HMS AMBUSCADE
   FROM COMMANDER TASK FORCE (Rear Admiral
   Woodward)
1. YOUR VALUABLE WORK AS AN ESCORT DURING
   CORPORATE HAS CONTRIBUTED SIGNIFICANTLY TO
   THE SUCCESS OF OUR OPERATIONS. THE 21 CLUB
   HAS FOUGHT HARD AND WELL.
2. BZ [well done] AND A HAPPY RUN HOME.
```

HMS Ambuscade.   *Heading north 8/7*

My darlingest, Hi, this will go off from Ascension, probably 15th! You will have more letters after this confirming dates, but we might possibly be back on Sat 24th in the morning – what we are hoping for, weather and Ascension Island programme permitting. Hooray!!! At last. Hope to go off on 3 weeks leave... Back on 16 Aug until 20 Sep in Devonport with Maintenance period. Then the big unknown.

Isn't that fabulous – much better than the late Autumn return and 10 days' leave. I don't know at all what the chances of us deploying again are, but fingers crossed that we won't (this ship was one of the few away last Christmas).

My darling, thanks for the card, which arrived before me at breakfast yesterday. Lovely thought, much appreciated. Please thank the children for theirs too. Louisa's was very good indeed.

My birthday was spent in South Georgia. Lunch onboard *Endurance* (TW aboard) and a 10-minute trip around a whaling station before returning. Spectacular scenery and well worth the visit if we had to go somewhere first!

Hard work seems to continue as we head north. Lots of more mundane things to do.

Thinking of you all the time (have more time to do so), and longing to get back. Make any arrangements you like for the hols – USA, HK... Wales?? I love you J

9th July
    Passage north, still negotiating icebergs
    in darkness. (Wind S, F2, SS3. 324 miles)

10th July
    Captain's Messdeck Rounds (formal
    inspection). Weather deteriorating
    rapidly, barometer fell 10mb in 30
    minutes. Winds off the scale over 60
    knots. Cracks in hull extending. (Wind SW,
    F9-12 violent storm, SS8 very high. 324
    miles)

Captain of HMS *Ambuscade*,
Commander Peter Mosse.

11th July
   Wind and sea coming around to west,
   remains above 30 knots for 36 hours.
   (Winds W, F10 storm, SS8. 366 miles)

12th July
   1545-1640 RAS(L) astern method with MV
   BRITISH ESK. Starboard Tyne main engine
   unserviceable, fuel pump broken. (433
   miles)

Calmer waters at last.
Royal Marine passengers watching the wake.

Westbourne, West Sussex.   *Monday, 12th July*

My darlingest one, I am hoping that this will get to you off Gibraltar, though I have been told that a mail pick-up there is only a possibility not a certainty, so I won't pour out my usual quantity of drivel! Isn't it exciting – you must be near Ascension now – perhaps even there. I guess you must be in company with Hermes, as SL told me privily that she was due back on 26th or so. Canberra returned yesterday to a Last Night at the Proms reception – balloons, Land of Hope and Glory, red roses, and in some cases an entire coach-load of people to meet <u>one</u> marine! Wee has broken up and brought home her work books and a very good report – she and Bee are up at the playschool this morning. My parents were brought down by Bim yesterday – it is now 10.30, and my mother is just getting up! Just what she needs, actually, as she is rather battered and bruised. Unfortunately the weather has turned thundery and very windy, so she can't just lie in the sun. But it doesn't rain, which would help the garden.

Eileen comes for lunch tomorrow, and we go to the theatre in the evening. Tea out on Wed, and a concert in the evening. Bim on Thursday, and Saturday I take them back, and Sunday we lunch out. A busy time that will fill up the enormous gap of time for the next fortnight. It seems so far away, and I do so long for it. It will be marvellous wherever we are, but I long to bring you home. All my love, J xxxx

13th July
   23 knot passage. Starboard Olympus main engine unserviceable. Starboard Tyne main engine fuel pump unserviceable. Village fete on Flight Deck; raised £555 for Falklands Fund. Advance clocks to Z time. (534 miles)

Village Fete,
raising money for Falklands Fund.

WEEKEND AT SEA

The weather having improved markedly, the ship held a Village Fete on the Flight Deck, with every type of stall available. We had a lot of fun and raised money for the South Atlantic Fund that had already been started in the UK for the families of those British servicemen and civilians who had lost their lives. While there were stalls that would be recognisable in any country village fete, there were a couple of unusual ones. We had collected a large bucket of soil and clod of turf from the Falkland Islands during one of the few boat sorties ashore, together with a tray of snow which was then stored in the freezer. I had decided while we were down in the Falklands to have a snowball fight as

Still bearded, the author poses with GPMG
and flak jacket, with a foot on Falklands' soil.

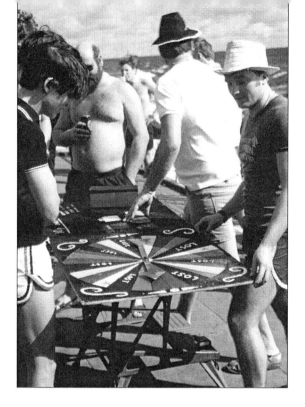

Flight Deck Casino.

we crossed the Equator going north. I sold snowballs at the Fete for £25 each for the Fund. These snowballs were to be thrown across the Equator from South to North, and I was hoping to get this feat into the Guinness Book of Records. I certainly was confident enough to guarantee to those 20-odd who purchased them that I would get their photograph into a national paper!

The turf we auctioned at the Village Fete, but only after it had served its purpose for photographic purposes. We mounted a machine gun on the temporary mounting we had constructed for the war, donned helmet and flak jacket, and had photographs taken of ourselves standing on Falklands soil – with the Union flag close by – posing as victors. It was, perhaps the only bit of outward triumph that we displayed throughout the whole saga, and then done in jest and at a cost of £5 a go. Many years later we learnt that the camera used by the Flight to take the photos of those dressed up in all the gear with the machine gun did not actually have any film in it. The SMR nearly got lynched when all those who had paid their fiver did not get any photos. At the time they were told that the film processing got lost at Boots but the truth came out at one of our reunions in Crewe.

As ever, Jack and Royal (affectionate names for sailors and Royal Marines) knew how to enjoy themselves and showed their characteristic generosity, raising £550 that afternoon. The following evening we barbecued on the Flight Deck and had sing-songs. Morale was good.

HMS Ambuscade.   13/7

Darlingest, First day of sun and tropical rig, and I shaved off today! Closer to Ascension, where we will get mail and send this off. We seem to be terribly busy at the moment – masses of reports, planning writing memos, accounting and so on. Not all work tho' – we had a mess dinner for leavers last night which went well (one leaves from Ascension), and this afternoon was a country fair on the flight deck raising money for widows of Type 21s. Raised nearly £600, which was stunning. Great fun had by all.

Still no exact date of our arrival back. Our engines are playing up and there's just a chance we may be delayed in As I while they fly some parts out. Should know tomorrow and obviously hope desperately not.

If all goes well, hope to get in on the morning of Sat 24th – could be delayed as late as Monday 26th. Then leave until 16 Aug. I can't wait for it – but will have to… Longing to see you. I wonder what your plans will be. Will you come down the night before? Probably have to park in car park at Drake (barracks) and get a coach down to the quay to meet us.   Hooray!

I hope to get away immediately and not come back! If we get in late morning there will probably be a buffet lunch – but I expect most or all will shoot through straight away. Especially if there are buses back to the car park. V. complicated not knowing what time we get in – or even exactly what day.   Advance leave party fly out of Ascension to have some leave and then take over duties once we get back.

My darling, I hope all is well with you. Take the greatest of care over these last few days. You are the most precious person on earth – look after yourself and don't overwork (I <u>do</u> want to come back to an overgrown garden and a scruffy house! – really!).

I love you and long for you. J

14th July
Helicopter unserviceable, tail cracked.
Barbecue on Flight Deck (Wind SE, F6, SS3.
500 miles)

HMS Ambuscade.   14/7

Darlingest J, V. quick note as we're sending helo into Asc this pm to collect our mail and a couple of passengers.

<u>Hopefully</u> our programme will be

Sat 24th July	Approx 0700	Enter Sound
		Anchor
		Customs
		TV?
		Up harbour
	10 15	Alongside

I expect you will be invited to park in Car park Drake 0915 –0945 with coach to jetty 0945... Will be telegramming you with a phone no. to ring to confirm ETA and details.

It is dependent on the receipt of 2 engine parts in Asc. – only signalled for yesterday, so if they don't arrive we will have to hang around for them... You can imagine – there's no requirement for an aircraft to bring them: the willpower of 200 ship's company is enough!!

Longing to see you, and to get mail. Hope to get another letter away from here tonight / tomorrow. Lots of love and to the children. I <u>have</u> shaved off, feel very slim and naked! No sun today in the trade winds.

See you soon – all my love J

SPEEDING HOME

Ascension reached, we landed M Company ashore, with our mail, and embarked sacks more of inbound mail. This was to be the last exchange of letters, for it had now become clear that we were homeward bound. A number of the ship's company was also landed, to be flown home for advanced leave. They would then be awaiting us on the jetty at Devonport ready to take over the duties onboard while the rest of us proceeded on leave.

15th July
> 0620 Anchor off Ascension Island, Vertrep stores. Land M Company 42 Commando. Fuel alongside MV ALVEGA, strawberries and cream delivered onboard! 1530 slip and proceed north for UK. Passage speed 22 knots. (Wind SE, F4, SS2. 201 Miles)

HMS Ambuscade.   *0600   15/7*

My honey, 12 letters from you ranging from 24th June to 7th July, hooray! VMT. Lovely to hear, don't write any more 'cos I'll be back hooray hooray. I've read them all quickly at about midnight last night and will work my way back thro' them in slower time later today. Just anchored off Ascension having got up at 0500 so it's going to be a long day. Humid but overcast, with dawn about to break.

I've asked our outgoing officer to give you a ring to explain anything that you're not quite clear about.

Leave: yes! I do plan to go on 3 weeks' leave immediately – at the same time as PM. Sat 24th to Mon 16th Aug. Uninterrupted – I hope! How about Wales for the mid week? Book now!! He always said the less notice the better – and lay on the war bit! Demand a good apartment – one of the ones with the funny baths!

Darlingest, delighted to hear that all is well with you and that

Leaving Ascension, heading north!

you have gorged yourself on garden vitamin C and that Alfonso is alive and kicking.

Delighted you got to Kensington Palace – sounds fun, but pity he was delayed. Glad L behaved herself.

I ought to write to both parents for Birthday cards, but haven't time. Please pass love and thanks.

Longing to see you. Take <u>greatest</u> care. See you, all being well, on Sat 24th. All my love, J

15/7

Dear Louisa and Marc, This is the last of these funny letters that I am going to write to you, because I'm on my way home. I am halfway there.

I am looking forward very much to seeing you both and hearing all about what you have been doing. Thank you both for your pictures which are excellent. Well done! Do some more for when I get back.

Ascension Island is a volcano in the middle of the sea – used by the moon buggy trials because it is so rocky.

Look after your marvellous Mummy. Lots of love, Daddy

CROSSING THE EQUATOR – AGAIN

After less than ten hours at Ascension we proceeded north yet again, anxious not to waste a single minute to get home. We spent much of our time squaring away the ship, getting our records and reports up to date, and keeping on top of our operational capabilities. There was time though for one formality that we had abandoned on our way south.

It is normal practice in a ship to hold an entertaining ritual with King Neptune holding court onboard when Crossing the Line. An ancient custom, it is great fun, but one should always do something to mark the occasion. On 9th May as we headed to war you may recall, we had stopped the ship on the Equator and had 'Hands to Bathe', so that sailors could swim across the Equator. Daily Orders had announced King Neptune's dispensation for this dereliction of duty.

On reaching the Equator this time, the ship duly stopped, and we lined up on the forecastle and threw the snowballs over the bow, above the head of (or was it at?) the photographer squatting in the eyes of the ship. It was more fun, and I am glad to say that the *News of the World* did publish the photograph, though the Guinness Book of Records declined us on some technical fault. We then embarked King Neptune, accompanied by Queen Amphitrite and his Court, comprising the Barber, Surgeon, policemen and bears. The full ceremony, with amusing charges read out against specific individuals, the administration of an evil-tasting medicine from the Surgeon together with a generous application of "shaving" foam from the Barber, is then followed by a riotous dunking in the large canvas pool built on

Throwing the snowballs made of Falklands' snow, across the Equator
for charity! Author far right of picture without beard.

the flight deck. Although in theory the ceremony is to initiate
members of the ship's company who have not previously crossed
the line, it is inevitable that key members are put on trial before
a general melee follows. Only those on watch are likely to escape!

16th July.
> Relaxed notice for weapons, sensors
> (radars, sonars, and electronic warfare
> receivers) at immediate notice
> Overflown by 2 Russian Bear D
> reconnaissance aircraft. 1430 Snowball
> fight across the Equator, then Crossing the
> Line Ceremony. Passage speed 18 knots.
> (Wind SE, F3, SS2. 485 Miles)

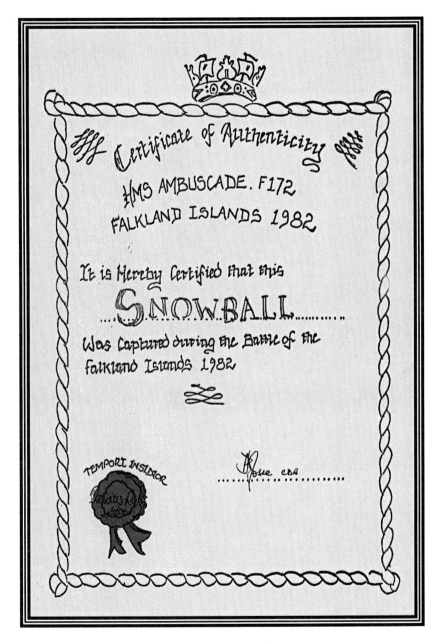

Falklands Snowball Certificate.

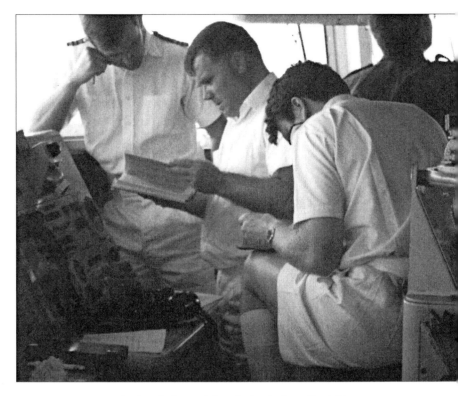

Author, Padre, and Captain (seated) on the bridge
checking a biblical quotation. Their tropical rig
makes a big change from the earlier action dress.

17th July
    Medical case of appendicitis onboard.
    Helicopter still unserviceable,
    "conservative treatment" only option.
    Passage speed 18 knots. (446 miles)

18th July
    Divert to Dakar because of medical
    emergency. RAS(L) RFA PEARLEAF. 2000-2200
    alongside to land patient. (Wind W, F3,
    SS4. 381 miles)

19 July

Fast passage into head winds and rough seas. Passage speed 21 knots. (Wind N, F5, SS5. 495 miles)

20th July

Fast passage continues. (Wind N, F4, SS4. 502 miles)

21st July

0850-1015 RAS(L) RFA PLUMLEAF. Last RAS of operation! Passage speed 25 knots then 21 knots. (Wind N, light, SS2. 464 miles)

22nd

Calm weather at last. Prepare for arrival in UK. Captain carries out formal Rounds (inspection) of the Supply and Secretariat Division areas of the ship. Passage speed 21 knots. (Wind W, F2, SS1. 458 miles)

23rd July

Captain's Rounds of the Operations Department. Flying Operations to receive stores. Fit new tail stabilizer to helicopter, then carry out Check Test Flight. 2200 Anchor in Plymouth Sound. (Wind N, light, SS3. 341 miles)

CHAPTER 15

HOMECOMING

Jenny's Viewpoint

KNOWING THAT John was on his way back was the best
tonic in the world, even though there was always the
uncomfortable thought that he might have to return to
patrol the islands. I was desperate to have him around at the
birth of Alfonso, as both the previous births had been prolonged
and difficult. However, one had to take the good days as they
came, and the idea of seeing John after all the danger and drama
that he had endured was a dream come true. If he had to go back
down south, we would have to face that later. The diversion via
South Georgia was something that I did not resent at all, since
everyone who had visited the island waxed lyrical about its
beauty – it had become a commonplace for wives to be amazed
at the purple passages about South Georgia in the letters they
received from husbands who had been there.

The night before *Ambuscade* arrived we spent with some
friends in Plymouth. Other wives, without children to get to bed,
were on the headland that night, listening for the sound of the
engines as the ship arrived in the dark, and anchored near the
breakwater, ready for the entry into harbour the next day. One of
them was a Wren, at that time a girlfriend, but later a wife. "Yes!"
she said on hearing the sound of a ship. "That is *Ambuscade*. I

Rust stained *Ambuscade*
entering Plymouth Sound.

know the sound of the Rolls-Royce engines!"

A kind friend (who became a godfather to Alfonso later in the year) took the three of us up to Devil's Point early in the morning, to see the ship coming in. It was a somewhat cloudy morning, but for us it was all sunshine. A reporter for the local Plymouth paper was there, wanting a story, and seeing us with our flags asked if he could take our photograph. "Are you connected with anyone on the ship?" he asked, and was delighted to find that we were. It seems that usually many local people had kindly come to welcome back the Task Force ships as they returned, making a great fuss of them. It was, however, bad luck on *Ambuscade* that her return clashed with something else in the Plymouth calendar, so the ship did not have the great parade up channel with the fire-hoses playing and the little ships cheering that so many of the earlier ships had had.

For us, however, it was a magical day. There was a moment of intense emotion as *Ambuscade*, rusty, weather-beaten and war-stained, rounded Drake's Island, and we could just about make out individuals through binoculars. It was such a pity they were all dressed alike! The children waved their flags wildly, and we thought we could recognize John – and then we had to get back into the car and dash for the dockyard, while the ship continued to make her slow way up the channel to the port. We parked at HMS *Drake*, the barracks attached to the dockyard, and got into

Nervous anticipation. Louisa and Marc wait on Plymouth Ho, with *Ambuscade* a mere blob in the harbour beyond.

Then excitement! Louisa and Marc greeting *Ambuscade* back to Plymouth Sound.

Passing Drake's Island in Plymouth Sound.

a bus to take us to the quayside. There the throng was, as one would have imagined, enormous, and enormously excited. As the ship slowly berthed alongside, everyone was shouting, waving, blowing kisses, jumping up and down, holding up new-born babies and little children – and then there was the business of setting up the gangways and securing the ship before we could go on board. That seemed to take forever and forever. The sizzling excitement was turning to exasperation and frustration – but suddenly it was done, and a tide of humanity, mostly wives and children, but also mums and dads, brothers, sisters and girlfriends, crowded onto the ship or absorbed with hugs the men pouring off. Astonishingly, we seemed to find our other halves almost immediately, and suddenly it was all over. The agony of the war, the waiting, the not knowing, the fears, the hopes, the anticipation and the stress was over. They were home.

24th July
0800 Embark Admiral to welcome HMS
Ambuscade home. 0815 Embark Press. 0830-
0900 Press Conference. Disembark our
helicopter to RNAS Portland. 0940
Disembark Admiral. 1000 weigh anchor,
proceed up harbour in Procedure Alpha (all
hands fallen in on upper deck in Number
One uniforms). 1030 Alongside in HM Naval
Base, Devonport. Families onboard. Ring
Off Main Engines. 47 hours notice. Press
disembark.

Anchoring in the most beautiful of harbours, Plymouth Sound, late in the evening of 23rd July, we cleaned up and prepared for entry into Devonport the following day. Before weighing anchor the next morning, the local admiral came out to greet us home on behalf of the Commander-in-Chief Fleet. I escorted him around the ship for a brief tour to meet the ship's company in their mess decks. One rather odd incident comes to mind which shows the tension of that morning. The Admiral and I were going down a passageway and, as I was about to hold a door open, a sailor barged through brushing the Admiral aside in a remarkably abrupt manner. Astonished, I called his name only to see him burst into tears and rush onto the upper deck. Emotions throughout the war had been kept in check and I had witnessed no tears until now. I suspect the man had received bad news from home, perhaps that his wife or girl friend would not be awaiting him on the jetty. Without comment, the Admiral continued his walk around. There followed a press conference onboard, but I remember little feeling of triumph, rather the frustration of just wanting to get back!

It should be noted that our helicopter had gone unserviceable on our passage north from Ascension Island because of a fault in

Families' view of *Ambuscade* coming alongside.

the tail stabiliser. A replacement was flown out to us as we arrived off Plymouth Sound and the Flight worked hard overnight to fit it. On this final morning, the Pilot and Observer, together with three members of the Flight, flew off to RNAS Portland to be greeted by their families at the Air Station at about the same time as we were completing the very last few yards of our homeward trip.

The final half hour passage into harbour was deeply memorable. Passing close to the rocky shore in the narrow entrance at Devil's Point, we could see families waving madly, and then as we manoeuvred alongside we could see our loved ones on the jetty. There were banners held aloft to welcome back individuals but it was hard to make out in the considerable crowd where our individual families were standing. Not that we could concentrate too much, for we had our work still to do to manoeuvre the ship alongside safely and handle the berthing hawsers. At long last I could see Jenny with little Louisa and Marc alongside her. The wait to get ashore was almost unbearable, for it takes time to crane the connecting ship's brow (the gangway) into position and then connect all the ropes and wires to keep it in position. But eventually there was that glorious moment when the ship's company could get ashore to hug – to laugh and cry

View from the bridge as we come alongside in Devonport.

with those who had meant so much to them over the preceding extraordinary experience.

What a remarkable day that was, and how much there was to talk about, on both sides. But somehow we then got on with our lives and resumed a normality that had appeared near impossible only a month before. We surprisingly quickly left the experience behind us, and lived for the future. I have not revisited those days in my memory, or through our letters, until now.

Looking aft to yet more families.

HMS *AMBUSCADE* VITAL STATISTICS

(To provide some interesting facts for the media at the Press Conference on the day of return, we provided this list of facts about *AMBUSCADE*'s individual statistics)

Miles steamed during Operation: 29,226
Continuous days at sea since Gibraltar: 83 days

MEDICAL
Patients seen : 101
Codeine pills issued: approx 200
Sea Sick pills issued: 480

MAIL RECEIVED: 106 sacks

POWER
Electricity used: 1,726,210 KW
Lamps (light bulbs) renewed: 2,500
Fuel used: 5044.76 tons
Replenishments (Liquid) at Sea: 25

Books of Reference amendments received: 780

Seacat missile tests: 249

COMMUNICATIONS
Teleprinter paper rolls used: 17,500 yards
Classified signals distributed: 19,128

HELICOPTER OPERATIONS
Helicopters used: 3
Hours flown: 167
Deck landings (not including other aircraft): 377

FOOD CONSUMED
Eggs: 20,000
Meat: 11,000 lbs
Chickens: 1,000
Sausages: 2,000
Baked Beans: 2,800 cans
Tomatoes: 2,000 cans
Milk: 10,800 pints
Potatoes; 33,000lbs
Baked bread: 2,500 loaves
                       12,000 rolls

NAAFI PURCHASES
Chocolate: 25,812 bars
Sweets: 28,880 bags
Soft drinks: 12,480 cans
Beer: 19,200 cans
Pot Noodles: 552
Crisps: 5,233 bags
Cigarettes: 345,000
Cigars: 3,350

AMMUNITION EXPENDED
4.5″ shells: 500
Torpedo: 1
Seacat missile: 1
Small arms: too many to count!

CHAPTER 16

POSTSCRIPT

T HE OFFICERS OF HMS *Ambuscade* gave their wives and girlfriends a traditional "Ladies' Night" dinner onboard in September that year and I, as the Wardroom Mess President, had to give the formal speech. After the opening words of welcome to the ladies and then the farewells to a number of officers who were about to leave us to take up new appointments, I then touched lightly on our recent experiences. These are extracts from that short speech:

"What a pleasure to say *"Ladies and Gentlemen"*. It has been a very long time since this mess has had the opportunity to gather for an occasion such as this, and for those who have joined us recently (and perhaps that includes even me!) – Welcome! Tonight is both a happy and sad occasion. Happy, in that we are still here, a whole ship (apart from our cracks!). We fought our war successfully and carried out our duties with honour. The friendships engendered by the experiences down south will be with us for life. But it is sad too, in that we are losing some of our friends so soon to go on to other appointments.

"Ladies, you are the unsung heroes – or rather, heroines of the South Atlantic. We have been only too aware of what you have been through over the last few months. While the war was never pleasant for us, we were at least aware of the actual danger around us and were constantly supported by the camaraderie onboard. For you, eight thousand miles away and often alone, there was the constant worry – and the mass of misinformation, be it from TV, radio, each other, or even the Families Information Bureau. (Did you know the latter were reporting that we were at the Chatham Navy Days when we were actually down south?!)

"For the support, encouragement, and love you sent us, and the fabulous welcome you gave us on our arrival back here in Plymouth, we thank you. This is your evening!"

Shortly afterwards, HMS *Ambuscade* sailed to Portland to carry out her 6 week Operational Sea Training programme, which had once been programmed to take place in May. It was hard work and not easy for any of us, despite our recent operational experience, for it all seemed rather petty and odd. But we completed it and passed our inspection. Instead of sailing south again to patrol in the Falkland Islands waters as we had earlier expected, we were despatched later East of Suez to carry out a seven month Armilla Patrol, guarding the oil routes out of the Gulf. While it was more separation from our loved ones, it was at least in more hospitable waters and sunshine.

When "Alfonso" was born in November, 1982, he was christened Oliver. The day Jenny was due to give birth, I left *Ambuscade* in Liverpool and hired a car to drive back to Westbourne. I made it in the nick of time to take her in to hospital and witness his birth but then had to rush back, before my wife Jenny even came round afterwards, to rejoin my ship to sail to Scotland. No paternity leave in those days! At the time of writing this, Oliver is a junior officer in the Scots Guards, the regiment we supported during the fighting and then took down to South Georgia. Jenny and I sometimes ponder what influences acted on his development through that extraordinary spring and summer of 1982.

On board HMS *Ambuscade* after we had finished the war and were heading home, there were many discussions about what the operation had meant for the long-term future of the Royal Navy. Firstly, there was the concern that the Navy would be split into two halves: those who had fought and those who had not.

Interestingly, history now shows that was not the case, either in the immediate aftermath of the war or over the years that followed. We personally were determined to avoid a "them and us" situation, and with the reasonably rapid change around of personnel within the ship's company, at all levels, the newcomers slotted in quickly and easily, and the old hands left to take their experiences on to new appointments. Certainly there was no bragging onboard about our efforts over the previous months.

Secondly, there was a renewed confidence that the draconian cuts that had been put into place by the Nott Defence Review of the previous year would be cancelled. Again, looking back over these twenty five years, the decommissioning of our aircraft carriers and amphibious capability was immediately halted. The Royal Navy today has a much increased amphibious reach and lift, and while only one aircraft carrier remains in full commission, there remain plans (at the time of writing this book, at least!) for two new enormously powerful aircraft carriers to replace the three Invincible Class that have served with such distinction for the last twenty five years or so. Until these are built there remains a question mark over the political will to invest so heavily in the defence of this country's vital interests.

Finally, we debated our operational capability as displayed by the operation. How good were we in reality? What were the lessons to be learned? Certainly Operation Corporate could be shown as a brilliant success for the UK Forces. The 8,000 mile supply line was one of the greatest challenges, but it worked. This was due to the hard work of tens of thousands of individuals who were not actually in the war zone, but who were just as vital to its success. The combined operation showed the armed forces working in close harmony, and their readiness and flexibility were most impressive. The operational training that had been rigorously pursued over previous years had paid dividends. The Royal Navy showed the wisdom of investing heavily in this training, and we were not found wanting. Yes, there were areas in which we could do much better, and these were picked up and acted upon. The loss of ships showed we could improve the design and materials used in construction and furnishing. Smoke had proved a real killer when ships had been hit, so there were measures to reduce the risk of acrid smoke being generated by materials used in the construction of the ships, and there were ways of controlling it built into the design. The new Type 23 frigate that was in the drawing stage in 1982 was radically changed to incorporate these lessons, benefiting enormously both in design and in armament.

Nine years later I was privileged to be Captain of the first of these, HMS *Norfolk*, and to command the Frigate Squadron of all Type 23 frigates. The confidence I had in her war-fighting capabilities was based on my experiences from down south. Later, in 1995, I became the Commodore of the School of Maritime Operations and ran the shore training of both officers and ratings at all levels, from junior ratings to Commanding Officers. Again, while some aspects of warfare had moved on, the efficacy of operational shore training in bringing together the team within the operations room proved itself a vital element of the Navy's fighting capability. Two years later I stepped up to take the duties of Flag Officer Sea Training, commanding the world-renowned organization responsible for getting the Royal Naval ships, and those of some twenty other nations, worked up to a state where they can fight and win. Throughout my time in this training role, my thoughts and ideals were based to a considerable degree on my experiences of 1982. Through the combined experience of very many individuals in the armed forces of the United Kingdom, the Falklands War has undoubtedly left a legacy of success for future generations to follow.

GLOSSARY

AOA   Amphibious Operating Area. The geographic area around San Carlos where the amphibious landing took place.

AGR   Anti Gas Respirator, more commonly known as a gas mask.

AWO   Above Water Warfare Officer

BFPO   British Forces Post Office

CBG   Carrier Battle Group. The main body of the naval forces off the Falkland Islands, based around the two aircraft carriers: HMS *HERMES* (the Flagship of Rear Admiral Woodward), and HMS *INVINCIBLE*.

CO   Commanding Officer, Captain of the ship.

CW   Chemical Warfare.

FDO   Flight Deck Officer.

FI   Falkland Islands.

First Lieutenant Executive Officer (XO),
       nicknamed The Jimmy and sometimes referred to as Number One.

FOST   Flag Officer Sea Training. The RN organization based at Portland which was responsible for all the sea training of RN ships – and those of several other nations as well.

Gunline   The geographical patrol line at sea, usually parallel to the coast, up and down which the ships would steam while firing their 4.5 inch guns in shore bombardment (see NGS).

LMA   Leading Medical Assistant, the right-hand man of the Surgeon Lieutenant onboard. However my letters refer to LMA as short for Louisa, Marc, and "Alfonso".

MEO   Marine Engineer Officer.

MO   Medical Officer.

NAAFI   Navy, Army and Airforce Institutes, the official trading organization serving the forces. On board ships, the NAAFI Manager and his assistant run a little multi purpose shop.

NATO   North Atlantic Treaty Organisation.

NBCD   Nuclear, Biological, and Chemical Defence. The NBCD State of the ship dictated the manning, and the NBCD Condition the material preparedness. Eg. NBCD State 1 Condition Zulu means that the Ship's Company are closed up at Action Stations and the ship has all doors and hatches fully closed and secured.

NGS   Naval Gunfire Support. Naval bombardment of shore targets.

OOW   Officer of the Watch, responsible for the safety of the ship and her company, navigating and conning the ship.

Pongos   Sailors' affectionate name for soldiers.

PWO   Principal Warfare Officer, responsible for fighting the ship.

RAF   Royal Air Force.

RAS   Replenishment at Sea. Underway replenishment between supplying ship (a tanker or stores ship) and other ships while steaming at normally 12 knots. (L) for liquids, normally fuel but sometimes water. (A) for ammunition, (S) for stores/solids.

RFA   Royal Fleet Auxiliaries. The tankers and stores ships, permanently attached to support the RN. 21 RFAs were deployed in support of the operation.

RNAS   Royal Naval Air Station.

SMR   Senior Maintenance Engineer of the Flight.

STUFT   Ships Taken Up From Trade. 54 ships were requisitioned from 33 companies to support the operation. The Merchant Navy played a vital and resolute part in the war.

TA   Transport Area. Previously named the AOA, this was the geographical area around San Carlos waters. Renamed after the landing was fully completed.

TEZ   Total Exclusion Zone, declared on 30 April as an area of 200 miles around the Falkland Islands to exclude all Argentine ships and aircraft.

TRALA   Tug, Repair and Logistic Area: a large holding area some 300 miles east of the Falklands, outside the range of enemy attack.

UAAI   Electronic Warfare Sensor.

U/S   Unserviceable; a formal way of describing broken equipment!

Vertrep Vertical Replenishment. Stores transferred by helicopter in underslung loads, on strops or in nets.

XO   Executive Officer (Second-in-Command). Yet another name for the First Lieutenant.

Zulu time Greenwich Mean Time.

BEAUFORT WIND SCALE

Beaufort Number	Descriptive Terms	Wind Speed Knots	Sea Conditions
0	**Calm**	1	Sea like a mirror.
1	**Light air**	1-3	Ripples.
2	**Light breeze**	4-6	Small wavelets.
3	**Gentle breeze**	7-10	Large wavelets; crests begin to break.
4	**Moderate breeze**	11-16	Small waves; fairly frequent white horses.
5	**Fresh breeze**	17-21	Moderate waves; many white horses.
6	**Strong breeze**	22-27	Large waves; some foam and spray.
7	**Near Gale**	28-33	Sea heaps up; white foam blown by wind.
8	**Gale**	34-40	Moderately high waves of greater length.
9	**Strong gale**	41-47	High waves; dense foam streaks, crests topple.
10	**Storm**	48-55	Very high waves with long overhanging crests; dense foam, whole sea takes a white appearance.
11	**Violent storm**	56-63	Exceptionally high waves; sea is completely covered in white foam patches.
12	**Hurricane**	>64	Air filled with foam; sea completely white with driving spray.

SEA STATE CODE

Code	Descriptive Terms	Height–Metres	Height–Feet
0	**Glassy calm**	0	0
1	**Rippled calm**	0-0.1	0-$1/2$
2	**Smooth**	0.1- 0.5	$1/2$-2
3	**Slight**	0.5-1.25	2-4
4	**Moderate**	1.25-2.5	4-8
5	**Rough**	2.5-4	8-13
6	**Very rough**	4-6	13-20
7	**High**	6-9	20-30
8	**Very high**	9-14	30-45
9	**Phenomenal**	Over 14	Over 45

INDEX

Jenny Lippiett.

John Lippiett.

Second Lieutenant Oliver Lippiett, Scots Guards
(centre, born November 1982)
at Sandhurst in 2006 after passing out parade.

———————————— THE LIPPIETT FAMILY ————————————

JOHN   LOUISA   OLIVER   JENNY   MARC